WALK
THIS WAY

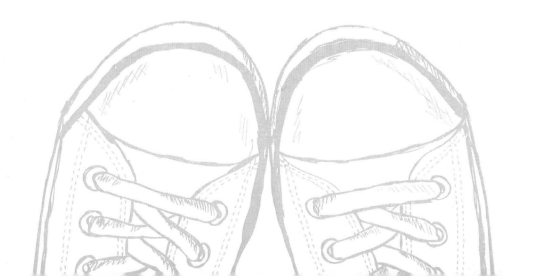

Walk This Way: Ethics and Sanctification Lessons for Kids

ISBN: 978-0-9981968-0-0

Publishing and Design Services: MelindaMartin.me

WALK THIS WAY

Ethics and Sanctification Lessons for Kids

ANNE MARIE GOSNELL

DEDICATION

■ ■

This book is dedicated to:

Eric, my husband, who has consistently encouraged me to
"get my stuff out there."

Vicki Pace, a dear friend, who tirelessly bugged me about
volunteering in Awana until I said, "Yes."

And to my Jesus, whom I love.

CONTENTS

■ ■ ■ ■ ■ ■ ■ ■ ■ ■ ■ ■ ■ ■ ■ ■ ■ ■ ■ ■

CONTENTS

INTRODUCTION

■■■■■■■■■■■■■■■■■■■■■■

Walk This Way: Ethics and Sanctification Lessons for Kids includes 20 interactive object lessons for children ages 5 to 12. These weekly lessons are meant to last 20-30 minutes. The terms *ethics* and *sanctification* are "churchy" words which mean to live as Jesus lived. Picture a child clomping around in his daddy's shoes. The shoes don't fit him, but the son longs to be like the father who wears them. As Christians, we are to "walk in Jesus' shoes" and be a light to the world. This means we must behave differently.

This curriculum will help you:

- teach engaging Bible lessons kids can't resist,

- create a fun teaching atmosphere that sparks the imagination of children,

- teach children Biblical truth that enhances their spiritual growth, and

- share the gospel and expand the Kingdom.

I am humbled that you have chosen to use this resource! I pray that it will ignite a passion for Jesus in those who hear you teach.

For more resources for parents and teachers, visit http://www.futureflyingsaucers.com/walk-way-resources-page/.

To receive weekly Bible lessons, book updates, and Children's Ministry helps, register directly at http://www.futureflyingsaucers.com.

Keep on keeping on, my friend!

Anne Marie Gosnell

FutureFlyingSaucers.com

And whenever you turn to the right or to the left, your ears will hear this command behind you: "This is the way. Walk in it."

—Isaiah 30:21

HOW THIS BOOK WORKS

■ ■ ■ ■ ■ ■ ■ ■ ■ ■ ■ ■ ■ ■ ■ ■ ■

I have put these lessons in an order that encourages spiritual growth. However, these lessons can be taught sequentially, or not. These lessons can be taught with large groups or small groups. When planning your Bible lessons, whether at home or church, figure out your objective first. Then look through the Table of Contents and decide which lessons will best help you reach your objective.

Each lesson has a **free downloadable poster** you can access from the **Resources Page (futureflyingsaucers.com/walk-way-resources-page)**. Display the posters in the room throughout this series and read them each week. You can choose to use them as memory verses. Other lesson freebies (game show cards, videos, printable pictures, etc.) can be found on the **Resources Page** as well.

Many lessons have a **Background** section. This summarizes the events that "set the stage" for the lesson. Use this section to help you put the lesson into context for the children.

The **Object Lesson** is usually first and might be referred to throughout the lesson. Most of the objects are items that many children know and see on a daily basis. Jesus used common objects such as sheep and trees when He taught, and we can do the same. Preparation time is minimal, and most lessons use materials you will find around your home. I do suggest practicing lessons ahead of time to be sure you understand how the activity works.

The **Bible Lesson** section is a paraphrase of the event from the **Scripture Focus**. Read the Scripture to prepare for teaching your lesson. Afterwards, read the Bible Lesson section a few times. Practice enough so that you can tell the story without reading.

The last section is important: **Life Application**. This is when Scripture "comes alive" and the kids learn how to apply it to their lives. If we do not explain the purpose of scripture to children, then you and I have failed as Bible teachers. All Scripture is useful, and we must showcase the glorious purpose of the Bible in each lesson.

At the end of each lesson is a **Comment Box**. That is an area for you to reflect about your teaching so you can improve your skills. Thinking retrospectively will help you to analyze your personal ministry. Ask yourself two questions: *"What went well as I taught this lesson?"* and *"What can I do better?"*

I'd love to know how your lessons go! Feel free to contact me at futureflying saucers@klopex.com. You can also join the **Facebook Group: Walk This Way Book (facebook.com/groups/173497166416848)**.

A FEW LAST TIPS

■ ■

Encourage the children to use their Bibles. Do not assume they think your story is Biblical because you tell it. Encourage them to be like the Bereans in the book of Acts. Show them in the Bible the verses you will be using. Some of the lessons will have the kids either reading along with you, or reading for themselves. If you have children who do not read, still help them find the reference in the Bible. This is a great habit to begin when young.

When you teach a lesson, try not to say words such as, *"Our story today comes from..."* While the Bible is the story of God, it is more than a story. We live in a world where the line between fairy tales, fiction, and truth is blurred. Because of this, refer to every person or event as history or biography. Children need to understand that people in Scripture were **real**, breathing people. The places in the Bible were—and some still are—**real** places.

Be enthusiastic when you teach. Do not put on a show, but share the joy of Jesus so that He is contagious! Scripture tells us that if Jesus is lifted up, He will draw all men to Him. Let us lift Him up!

One last thing: NEVER be afraid to share your testimony! Someone in the room might need to hear how God has worked in your past, how He is working today, and what He is doing in your future.

1 ACCEPT ADVICE AND INSTRUCTION

■ ■

Why is it that we have such a hard time accepting advice and instruction? Pride? Arrogance? Self-righteousness? This lesson will explore the Bible story of Rehoboam and what happened when he refused sound advice. Being able to handle correction with a good attitude will help our children take a step in the right direction on the narrow path of godliness {Deuteronomy 5:32}.

Scripture Focus: 1 Kings 12:1-20

Materials:

• Blindfold

• Chair

• Proverbs 10:17 poster

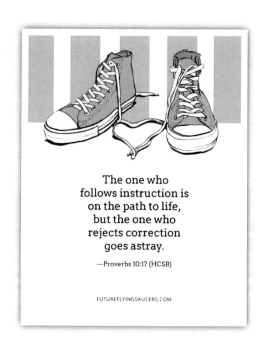

The one who follows instruction is on the path to life, but the one who rejects correction goes astray.

—Proverbs 10:17 (HCSB)

FUTUREFLYINGSAUCERS.COM

Background: 1 Kings 11 tells us about Solomon, including some bad choices he made. It also explains that Jeroboam was Solomon's servant. Ahijah was the prophet who told Jeroboam that the nation of Israel was going to split and ten tribes would make him the king. Because of the prophecy, Solomon wanted to kill Jeroboam. Jeroboam fled to Egypt for safety.

OBJECT LESSON

■ ■ ■ ■ ■ ■ ■ ■ ■ ■ ■ ■ ■ ■ ■ ■ ■ ■ ■

{Choose a child to leave the room and put on a blindfold. Tell the remaining children that they will be giving instructions to the blindfolded child, directing him to a chair and to sit down. They are not allowed to use the word *chair*.

Have the blindfolded child enter the room. Tell him to listen well and that he will not be led astray. Have the children give the directions as the blindfolded one follows.}

{Once the child is in the chair, ask:}

- Was it easy or hard to listen?

- Did you trust the information being given to you?

- Why or why not?

- Did you succeed or not?

{NOTE: I had one class that succeeded and one that failed. It made for interesting discussion. If the child does not make it to the chair, ask those who gave the directions, *"What could you have done better?"*}

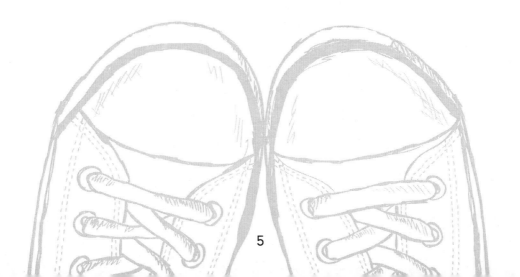

5

BIBLE LESSON

■ ■

Chapter 12 of 1 Kings tells us that King Solomon died and his son Rehoboam was made king. Jeroboam, who had fled from King Solomon, was urged to come back by the people of Israel.

Jeroboam and the people stood before Rehoboam and said, *"Your father was very hard on us. Please lighten the load of service and we will serve you."* Rehoboam told Jeroboam and the people to give him three days to think about it.

King Rehoboam consulted his father's old, wise men, the elders. Their advice: *"Lighten the load and the people will serve you forever!"*

King Rehoboam refused this advice and turned to the young men, his friends with whom he had grown up. Their advice: *"Tell the people that your little finger is thicker than your father's waist!"*

Three days later, Jeroboam and the people stood before King Rehoboam. The king answered the people roughly and did not listen to the elders. When this happened, the people responded with, *"To your tents, O Israel!"*—which meant, *"Revolt!"*

The people followed Jeroboam and not the king. Only the tribe of Judah stayed with King Rehoboam. The other ten tribes split and became the nation of Israel. The prophecy had come true.

LIFE APPLICATION

■ ■ ■ ■ ■ ■ ■ ■ ■ ■ ■ ■ ■ ■ ■ ■ ■ ■ ■

King Rehoboam was a new king. The young men were also new to kingdom leadership. When you are "new" to something, you do not know how to do it well. You need to learn.

The elders had been around a while. The elders had advised King Solomon, who was Rehoboam's father, and they had years of leadership experience and wisdom.

When the blindfolded person was being given directions, he had to listen carefully and then follow what was said, or he would fail.

{Ask:}

- Did Rehoboam succeed or fail as a king? [*Failed*]

Rehoboam did not listen to the correct advice and he failed. **The same thing can happen to you.** Your elders (parents, teachers, Sunday school leaders, church leaders) have been around a while and are experienced with life. Even better, they WANT to see all children succeed. They WANT to see you walk the path of godliness that Jesus set up for us.

This is only possible if you have decided to make Jesus your Lord and Master. Salvation is not the end to having a Christian life. Baptism is not the end. All of that is just the beginning. God wants to turn each person into the image of Jesus, and He does that by making you more *godly*, or "more like God." This is something God wants to do every day.

The only way He can work on our hearts and help us "walk a straight path to the chair" is for us to listen to Him. God speaks through the Bible and through our elders. At times, He can speak to you through friends your own age. However, they are new to life as well, so you have to be careful.

{Hold up the poster. Read it aloud.}

Proverbs is great at showing choices.

{Ask:}

- What are the two choices in this verse? [*Follow instruction or rejects instruction.*]

7

- What happens if we listen and follow instruction? [*We are on the path of life*.]

- What happens if we refuse instruction? [*We will go astray*.]

- What does "astray" mean? [To move away from the correct path]

You must decide.

What can we learn from Rehoboam? If we want to be godly, we must be sure to listen to the right advice and instruction.

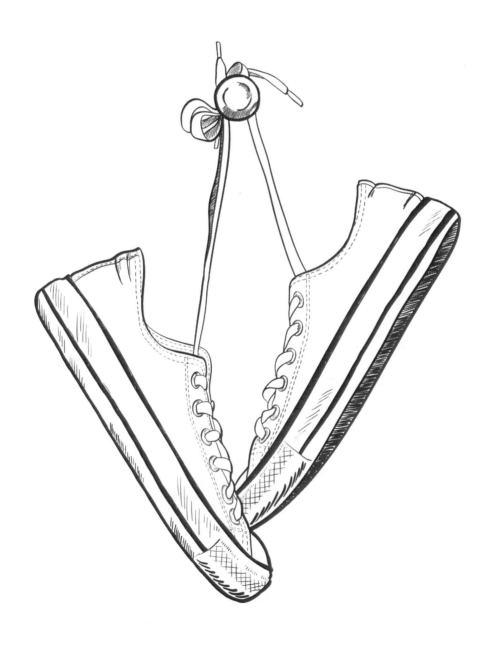

COMMENT BOX

■ ■ ■ ■ ■ ■ ■ ■ ■ ■ ■ ■ ■ ■ ■ ■ ■ ■ ■

THINK: What went well as you taught this lesson? What can you do better?

_____

_____

_____

_____

_____

_____

_____

_____

TIP: How are you at accepting advice? As you teach the lessons in this book, allow yourself to be trained. Not only will you become a better teacher, but you will become a better child of God.

2 DEALING WITH BAD LANGUAGE

■ ■

Bad language is more than using words that are inappropriate. Helping our children understand that bad language can be harmful to themselves and others is a step in the right direction on the narrow path of godliness. {Deuteronomy 5:32}

Scripture Focus: James 3:1-10 (*The Message*)

Materials:

But no man
can tame the tongue.
It is a restless evil,
full of deadly poison.
We praise our Lord and Father
with it, and we curse men who are
made in God's likeness with it.
Praising and cursing come
out of the same mouth.
My brothers, these things should
not be this way.

—James 3:8-10 (HCSB)

FUTUREFLYINGSAUCERS.COM

- Old placemat

- 3 empty tea bags (cut off the top and dump out the tea)

- Scissors

- Utility lighter for kitchens or camping

- Picture of a horse with a bridle (See Resources Page. If you have a real bridle that would be even better!)

- Picture of a ship's rudder (See Resources Page.)

- Fire extinguisher (just in case)

- James 3:8-10 poster

See the Resources Page for a video that shows what the tea bag rocket will do. Be sure to practice this a few times. Have extra empty tea bags as backup if any of the three you have fail.

BIBLE AND OBJECT LESSON

■ ■

{Have the placemat on the table in front of you, but do not put anything else on it. Have your pictures nearby.}

{Ask:}

- What do you think of when I say, "Bad language"? [*Allow answers. Make sure you tell the kids not to actually SAY any bad words. Lead the discussion to include words that might hurt another person, lying words, manipulative words, and gossip.*]

God has a lot to say about our tongues. Most of it is not good.

{Hold up the picture of the horse. Explain where the bridle is and what it does. Then hold up the picture of the ship rudder and explain how the direction of the ship changes with the movement of the rudder.}

The bridle is small compared to the horse. The rudder is small compared to the ship. Our tongues are small compared to the rest of our bodies; however, Scripture tells us that it causes the most damage.

{Read James 3:1-10. I really like *The Message* version of these verses on page 485. Skip the first five sentences and read to the beginning of the last paragraph.}

{Ask:}

- So what can our tongues be like? [*A bridle, a rudder, a small flame*]

- What happens when a bridle does not work correctly? [*The horse won't do what the rider wants.*]

- What happens when a rudder does not work correctly? [*The ship could run aground and wreck.*]

- Where do we see tame animals? [*The circus, the zoo, amusement parks*]

- What tame animals have you seen before? [*Dogs, cats, birds....may expand into tigers, elephants, whales, and seals*]

- What does it mean that those animals are tame? [*The animals will do what their master wants them to do.*]

- Can we tame the tongue? [*No*]

{Place the tea bag upside down on the placemat.}

The book of James has given us quite a few word pictures about our tongues. Our tongues are like the bridle of a horse and the rudder of a ship. Our tongues can give directions or cause damage. Our tongue can also be like a small flame.

{Light the tea bag. It should burn and the last little bit of the bag should fly quickly into the air with the last of the flame and disappear.}

LIFE APPLICATION

One little flame can burn down an entire forest, but this flame flew for a moment and disappeared. That is what our words do. They fly out of our mouths quickly, and then the words are gone and you can never get them back.

Every bad word you say, every hurtful word you say, or every bit of juicy gossip you say can never be returned to you. Your words can either cause good or they can cause damage.

{Hold up the poster. Read it aloud.}

People can tame all kinds of wild animals, but we have a hard time taming the tongue. It will be THE hardest thing for you to control. One moment you might be blessing God with your mouth, and the next moment you might be saying a mean thing about a friend.

What do you do?

You must remember that every person is created in God's likeness, the image of God. When you speak poorly of another person, you are speaking about someone God created for a special purpose. You are insulting God. Every person is valuable whether you see the value or not.

Be careful with what you say. You cannot take your words back. No amount of apologies or forgiveness can change what you said, although you should apologize and ask forgiveness. Later in the book of James, he talks about reputation. You will not have a good reputation if you use bad language.

What can you do if someone around you uses bad language? It is fine to ask them to not speak that way around you. It might be a hard thing to do, and they might turn some harsh words your way, but in the end, doing the right thing is better than being surrounded and tempted by sin.

What can we learn from the book of James? If we want to be godly, we must watch our words or we might end up hurting ourselves or others.

COMMENT BOX

■ ■

THINK: What went well as you taught this lesson? What can you do better?

_____

_____

_____

_____

_____

_____

_____

_____

_____

_____

TIP: The children will want you to do this trick again for them! If you do, be sure to reinforce the fact that words disappear just as the flame disappears.

3 ENCOURAGE COURTEOUS BEHAVIOR

■ ■

Many people do not realize it, but Jesus spoke about heaven quite a bit. In one of His sermons, He teaches us that certain behaviors are required in order to enter heaven. Encouraging courteous behavior will help our children take a step in the right direction on the narrow path of godliness. {Deuteronomy 5:32}

Scripture Focus: Matthew 25:31-46

Materials:

FUTUREFLYINGSAUCERS.COM

- Game Show Cards (See Resources Page.)

- Matthew 25:40 poster

See the Resources Page for video tips for this lesson.

Background: During the last few weeks of Jesus' life, He took the disciples aside to teach them. There were so many things they needed to know and so many questions that needed answered.

Truly, I say to you, to the extent that you did it to one of these brothers of Mine, even the least of them, you did it to Me.

—Matthew 25:40 (NASB)

One day, while Jesus sat on the Mount of Olives, the disciples came to Him and asked, *"What will be the signs of when you will be returning?"* From that question, Jesus begins a long teaching about the end times, the Tribulation, the Second Coming, heaven, and the Judgment.

COURTESY GAME SHOW

■ ■ ■ ■ ■ ■ ■ ■ ■ ■ ■ ■ ■ ■ ■ ■ ■ ■

{If you happen to have an adult volunteer who has a fantastic "game show voice," ask him/her to help you play this game with the kids.}

1. Cut apart the Game Show Cards and give them to your "game show host."

2. Divide the children into two equal groups. You can have the children number off 1, 2, 1, 2…or some other random way. Name one group the "sheep" and the other group the "goats."

3. Tell the sheep that no matter what question is asked of them, their answer will always be, "*Yes!*" Tell the goats that no matter what question is asked of them, their answer will always be, "*No!*"

4. Pretend you are the game show host, unless you have a volunteer. You can really have a lot of fun with it!

5. Read the first question. Point to one group for the answer. Then point to the other group. Each group should respond with the assigned answer.

6. Continue with all eight questions.

7. At the end, ask, "*Who wins? The sheep or the goats?*"

BIBLE LESSON

{Once the children have settled down, read Matthew 25:31-46 to them.}

{Ask:}

- Where will the Son of Man sit? [*On the throne of glory*]

- Who will be with the Son of Man? [*The holy angels*]

- Who is the Son of Man? [*Jesus*]

- What is gathered around in front of Him? [*All the nations*]

- Does that include you? Are you a part of a nation? [*Yes*]

- What will Jesus do with the nations? [*He will separate them and put the sheep on His right and the goats on His left.*]

- What had the sheep done? [*These fed the hungry, gave water to the thirsty, helped strangers, clothed the naked, helped the sick, and visited those in prison.*]

- What had the goats done? [*Nothing*]

- What is the reward for the sheep? [*They will inherit the kingdom—eternal life.*]

- What is the punishment for the goats? [*These will go into the everlasting fire prepared for the devil and his angels.*]

LIFE APPLICATION

■ ■

{Hold up the poster. Read it aloud.}

{Ask:}

- Who wins the game show—the sheep or the goats? [*The sheep*]

- Doing all those nice things and being courteous to others, does not **give** us eternal life. What does John 3:16 say? [*Have the kids quote it if possible*.]

Believing in Jesus is what gives us eternal life. Good works will not save you, but the book of James tells us that faith without works is dead. John 6:29 tells us that the first work of God is for us to believe in Jesus. If a person REALLY does believe in Jesus and desires to live a godly life, then courteous behavior will be seen. Because we believe in Jesus and want to live for Him, we will do good things.

However, if a person disobeys his/her parents, uses bad words, knocks over his brother, cheats on a test, causes strife, is difficult in all things all the time...and then claims to love Jesus, that person is called a hypocrite.

If you claim to be a Christian, you are to act "Christ-like." **You are to attempt to be godly.** Does that mean you will never mess up or never sin? Absolutely not! When you do mess up, you ask for forgiveness from God and any others you have wronged, and try not to do it again.

Hell is a real place. Jesus will separate the nations into two groups. You have to decide if you are a goat or a sheep. When you help other people, you are helping Jesus. When you choose NOT to be courteous to others, you are NOT being courteous to Jesus.

If you believe in Jesus, but you are acting like a goat, change your ways!

What can we learn from the sheep and the goats? If we want to be godly, we must choose to be courteous and help others.

COMMENT BOX

■ ■ ■ ■ ■ ■ ■ ■ ■ ■ ■ ■ ■ ■ ■ ■ ■ ■ ■ ■

THINK: What went well as you taught this lesson? What can you do better?

_____

_____

_____

_____

_____

_____

_____

_____

_____

TIP: Remind the children that you have been playing a game, but that there is a serious point to the game. Also, as the kids begin to understand the Bible truth, be sure to tell those who were "goats" that you are not saying they are "goats that are going to hell." The children might become concerned that they are going to hell because they were a "goat" in the game.

4 BECOME A SECRET INITIATIVE SERVANT

■■■■■■■■■■■■■■■■■■■■■■■■

We are told that we should do random acts of kindness. Why? Helping our children know how to take the initiative is a step in the right direction on the narrow path of godliness. {Deuteronomy 5:32}

Scripture Focus: 2 Kings 22 and 23

Materials:

- Binoculars or a spyglass

- James 4:17 poster

So it is a sin for the person who knows to do what is good and doesn't do it.

—James 4:17 (HCSB)

FUTUREFLYINGSAUCERS.COM

Background: In Second Kings, the nation of Judah had been warned that their punishment was coming. They had strayed and rebelled against the Lord long enough.

King Hezekiah was gone. He was a king that, though not perfect, desired to "do what was right in the sight of the Lord." Then came his son Manasseh, who is still known to be the most evil king who ever lived.

Manasseh's son, Amon, did evil in the sight of the Lord. His servants went against him and killed him. That placed Amon's eight-year-old son, Josiah, on the throne.

OBJECT LESSON

■ ■ ■ ■ ■ ■ ■ ■ ■ ■ ■ ■ ■ ■ ■ ■ ■ ■ ■

{Hold up the binoculars to your eyes and look at the kids.}

{Ask:}

- What are these and what do they do? [*Allow us to see farther away; make things larger so we can see them*]

- What might we use these for? [*Bird watching, use on a ship to watch for land, etc.*]

Sometimes people will use binoculars to watch other people. Think of spies. They watch from a far distance to see what people might be doing.

I am going to teach you to use your hearts' binoculars so you can be a **Secret Initiative Servant**!

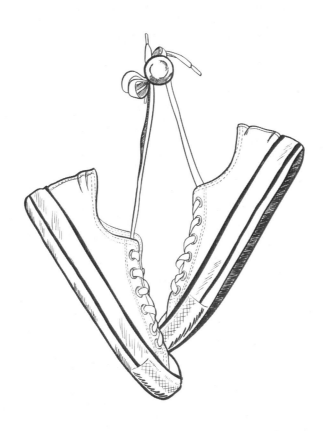

BIBLE LESSON

■ ■

In the Old Testament, the nation of Israel split into two kingdoms. Israel was the Northern Kingdom and Judah was the Southern Kingdom. This event took place in Judah, the Southern Kingdom.

King Josiah was eight years old when his father was killed and he became king. The Bible has a great verse about him if you read **2 Kings 22:2**:

"He did right in the sight of the Lord and walked in all the ways of his father David, nor did he turn aside to the right or to the left."

Wow! He must have really loved the Lord. This is interesting because of what happened next.

When he was 18, King Josiah sent a scribe to the high priest. The scribe told the high priest to have the temple repaired. The people of Judah had been rebellious during his father's and grandfather's reigns; therefore, the temple was falling into ruin. Josiah wanted to fix that.

While the temple was being improved, the high priest found a book. He had it taken to the king. The scribe read the book to King Josiah.

When King Josiah heard the words of the book, he ripped his clothes, which was a sign of grief and distress. The book was the Law of God. Because of the evil choices of the people, the Law of God had been lost in the temple.

It is interesting that Josiah somehow knew about God and His ways, but the scrolls of the Bible had been lost. I wonder if he had a mom or a teacher who taught him the ways of God.

Josiah had the scribe and high priest go to a prophetess to find out what Judah's punishment would be for their reckless behavior. Huldah told the men that calamity would take place in Judah. However, because of Josiah's heart for God, the destruction would not happen during his lifetime.

When Josiah heard this, he gathered all the people at the temple and vowed before them that he would follow the Lord and keep His commands with all his heart. Because of his leadership, all of the people followed his example.

Josiah knew what had to happen. Judah had to be cleaned up. Josiah ordered idols taken down and smashed. There were even idols in the temple that were taken out and burned. He destroyed anything that defiled the kingdom. He ordered that the priests go through a cleansing to make them right with God again so they could serve in the Temple. There were pillars and smaller temples that had been built throughout the kingdom, and Josiah had those torn down. He also executed the evil priests.

Once all of this was done, King Josiah commanded the people to keep the Passover feast. They had a grand party worshiping the Lord!

LIFE APPLICATION

When you look through binoculars, they help your eyes see well. That is what God's Law does for us. It helps our eyes and hearts to see what is going on around us.

When King Josiah read the Law, he knew he had to do the right thing. He knew he had to get Judah cleaned up. He knew the Temple needed to be cleansed. He knew the people would go back to the pillars and temples if he did not get rid of them. He knew the people needed to celebrate the Passover and go back to worshiping in the Temple.

What if he knew what to do and didn't do it?

{Hold up the poster. Read it aloud.}

If you see something that needs to be done because it is the right thing to do, and don't do it, you have sinned. So how can you do better? You do the right thing! This is when you become a **Secret Initiative Servant**.

"Taking the initiative" is doing something without being told. A **Secret Initiative Servant** is someone who secretly watches what is going on around him and then takes the initiative to help whenever he can.

If you want to be an amazing **Secret Initiative Servant**, do something good for someone secretly. They might figure out you did it, but they might not. That is the fun that comes from being a **Secret Initiative Servant**.

{Ask:}

- What are some ways we can be **Secret Initiative Servants**? [*Allow for answers.*]

What can we learn from King Josiah? If we want to be godly, we must choose to do what needs to be done because it is the right thing to do.

COMMENT BOX

■ ■

THINK: What went well as you taught this lesson? What can you do better?

_____

_____

_____

_____

_____

_____

_____

_____

_____

_____

TIP: Some children really become excited about becoming a Secret Initiative Servant! Capitalize on that by having the kids tell you the next week one of the secret things they did. Some may tell you anyway without being asked!

5 CHOOSE TO BE A PEACEMAKER

■ ■

Jesus said, *"Blessed are the peacemakers."* What exactly does that mean? When Jesus was here on earth, things were not very peaceful around Him. Helping our children know how and when to be peacemakers is a step in the right direction on the narrow path of godliness. {Deuteronomy 5:32}

Scripture Focus: Mark 11:15-18; Matthew 26:47-56

Materials:

- Picture of a dove (See Resources Page)

- Romans 12:18 poster

Background: Jesus returned to Jerusalem knowing that it would be the last week of His life. He entered the city on a donkey to the cheers of the people. But He wept for them because He understood their hearts. He knew they needed to be saved, not from Rome, but from sin. Jesus took sin seriously.

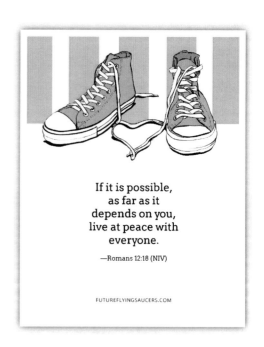

If it is possible,
as far as it
depends on you,
live at peace with
everyone.

—Romans 12:18 (NIV)

FUTUREFLYINGSAUCERS.COM

OBJECT LESSON

■ ■

{Show the picture of the dove.}

{Ask:}

- What do you know about doves? [*Allow answers.*]

- When do doves appear in Scripture? [*Allow answers: Noah and the ark, Jesus' baptism, doves were sold in the temple for sacrifice.*]

Here is some information that you might not know about doves. There are a lot of doves. They live all over the world except in the Sahara Desert and Antarctica. Doves are peaceful animals. While other birds might swoop and attack trying to keep predators away from their nests, doves keep to themselves. They can easily be handled by people. They can be trained and kept as pets.

Doves are a symbol of peace because they do not cause strife, or trouble, with anyone or anything. They can build a nest in many different places, eat their seeds, and live life in peace.

BIBLE LESSON

{Ask:}

- Was Jesus a peacemaker? [*Allow the kids to think and answer. Do not react. They will probably vacillate between answers.*]

Jesus tells us to be peacemakers when He preaches about the Beatitudes. There are two events that took place that we need to think about.

The first event was when Jesus went into the Temple and chased out the money changers. **{Read Mark 11:15-18.}** That does not sound very peaceful. Let's question this.

{Ask:}

- Where was Jesus? [*In Jerusalem at the Temple*]

- Why did people come to the Temple? [*To worship God*]

- What did Jesus do this time when He entered the Temple? [*He drove out those who were selling in the Temple, overturned the tables of the money changers, and would not allow those with something to sell to carry their items through the Temple.*]

- Did Jesus explain why He did what He did? [*Yes; the temple was to be a place of prayer and those people had turned it into a den of robbers.*]

- How did the scribes and priests respond to Jesus? [*They wanted to figure out how to destroy Him; they feared Him.*]

- What did the people think about Jesus? [*They were astonished by His teaching.*]

That does not sound so peaceful. What about this second event?

{Read Matthew 26:47-56.} Now let's question this.

{Ask:}

- Where was Jesus? [*In the Garden of Gethsemane*]

- Who came with Judas and what did he do? [*A multitude of people came with him, and he kissed Jesus.*]

- What happened when they tried to arrest Jesus? [*Someone took a sword and cut off the ear of the servant of the high priest.*]

- How did Jesus respond? Did He tell them to fight? [*No, He said for the sword to be put away and that those who fight by the sword will die by the sword.*]

- What extra information do we find in Luke 22:51? [*Jesus healed the man's ear that had been cut off.*]

Does this sound peaceful? Yes, and no.

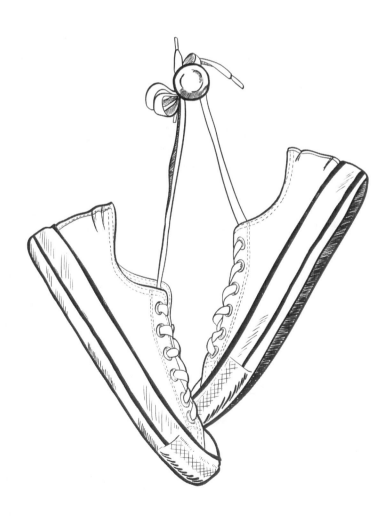

LIFE APPLICATION

■ ■ ■ ■ ■ ■ ■ ■ ■ ■ ■ ■ ■ ■ ■ ■ ■ ■ ■ ■

One of the names of Jesus is *Prince of Peace*. In the events read for this lesson, there does not seem to be much peace surrounding Jesus. In the Temple, He was the one causing the trouble. In the Garden of Gethsemane, the mob and the disciples created chaos.

{Ask:}

- What is peace? What does it mean to be a peacemaker since Jesus tells us to be one? [*Allow for answers.*]

A peacemaker is a person who creates a quiet environment and good relationships with other people. People who are filled with peace do not suffer from oppressive or negative thoughts and emotions on a regular basis.

{Ask:}

- Did Jesus do these things? [*Allow for answers.*]

{Hold up the poster. Read it aloud.}

The Scripture from Romans tells us, if it is possible, we are to live at peace with everyone. So when should we NOT be at peace with people?

Did Jesus purposely go around causing trouble just so He could cause trouble, or was He honorably reacting to the sin of others? In the Temple, He responded to the sin of those people who had disgraced the Temple. In the Garden of Gethsemane, He asked for the sword to be put away because that was not the correct way to respond to the sin in that situation.

{Read Matthew 26:52-56.}

{Ask:}

- For what purpose was everything happening to Jesus? [*So Scripture would be fulfilled*]

In all situations we need to make sure that we are not the ones causing trouble. We should be at peace with people. If we do something wrong, we need to be sorry for what we did and apologize. We need to be at peace with God, which is why Jesus had to die on the cross. If you do not believe in Jesus, you are not at peace with God.

When should we fight? Jesus fought against sin and loved the people involved. So if something is happening around us, and it is based on sin, we need to stand up and fight for what is righteous and also love the people who are involved.

What can we learn from Jesus when He was in the Temple and the Garden of Gethsemane? If we want to be godly, we must choose peace in all situations, unless righteousness is being overtaken by sin.

COMMENT BOX

■ ■

THINK: What went well as you taught this lesson? What can you do better?

_____

_____

_____

_____

_____

_____

_____

_____

_____

_____

TIP: Know that you ARE making a difference in the lives of your children! You may not see evidence today, but the Word of God is active and will produce fruit one day.

6 DEALING WITH TEMPTATION

■ ■

Have you ever been tempted to do something wrong? Have you ever tried to hide something you did? This Bible lesson focusing on Elisha's servant, Gehazi, will help our children understand that relying on God to help them conquer temptation is a step in the right direction on the narrow path of godliness. {Deuteronomy 5:32}

Scripture Focus: 2 Kings 5:14-27

Materials:

- See Resources Page for *The Marshmallow Test* video.

- Bag of large marshmallows

- 1 Corinthians 10:13 poster

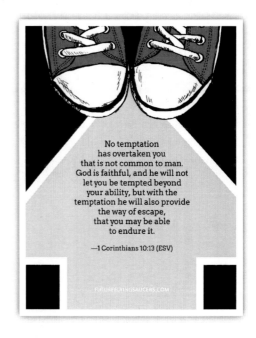

No temptation has overtaken you that is not common to man. God is faithful, and he will not let you be tempted beyond your ability, but with the temptation he will also provide the way of escape, that you may be able to endure it.

—1 Corinthians 10:13 (ESV)

FUTUREFLYINGSAUCERS.COM

Background: Elisha was a prophet. He was beloved by the people of Israel, and God used him in mighty ways. Naaman was a commander of the army of the nation of Syria. Syria and Israel were enemies, but Commander Naaman had a servant girl who was from Israel. Naaman ended up contracting leprosy, which is awful. Not only is leprosy a bad disease, but it also brings about great fear because of how it spreads. In Bible days, people would be told to leave their families and towns, and they would go live in the wilderness in leper colonies. This little girl didn't want that to happen to her master, so she told him about Elisha, the prophet of Israel. This lesson is not the story of Naaman, although he is a part of this event. Naaman is healed by God through Elisha's leadership, and this temptation lesson begins as Naaman is about to leave.

OBJECT LESSON

■ ■

{Pull out a marshmallow.}

{Ask:}

- What is this? Do you like marshmallows? [*Allow for answers.*]

- What would you do if you were put in an empty room and given a marshmallow? Would you eat it? [*Allow for answers.*]

- What if you were put in an empty room and were told this when you were given the marshmallow: *"Here is a marshmallow. I am going to leave the room for a little while. You can eat this marshmallow, BUT if you do not eat it while I am gone, I'll give you another one when I return. Then you will have two."* What would you do? [*Allow for answers.*]

{Show the video *The Marshmallow Test*.}

That marshmallow was a temptation to those kids!

{Ask:}

- What did most of them do? [*Waited for the second marshmallow*]

They knew that something better was coming, and they wanted to wait for it instead of eating the one marshmallow right away.

BIBLE LESSON

Through Elisha, God healed Naaman. After he was healed, Naaman wanted to thank Elisha and offered him all kinds of money, clothes, and treasures. Elisha told Naaman that he would take nothing. Naaman urged him, but Elisha refused.

Elisha's servant, Gehazi, thought differently. He wanted some of that good treasure. He became tempted by it. Instead of turning away and moving on, he decided to sin.

Naaman's caravan had already left. Gehazi started running, and he caught up to Naaman. Naaman stopped and asked if everything was ok.

The problem with sin is that once you begin with one sin, it usually snowballs into more sin and more sin. Gehazi told Naaman that everything was fine, but that Elisha had sent him to ask for just a few things because two young men from the sons of the prophets had arrived. Would Naaman be willing to give one talent and two changes of clothes?

Naaman agreed. In fact, Naaman gave two talents instead of only one. He also sent two servants back with Gehazi so he would not have to carry anything. Once Gehazi and the servants reached Elisha's home, the servants left and Gehazi hid the money and clothes. Gehazi then went to see Elisha.

Elisha asked, "*Where did you go, Gehazi?*" Gehazi responded by saying that he did not go anywhere. Elisha then stated, "*Do you not understand that my heart went with you? Do we really need all of those riches? Now the leprosy of Naaman will be upon you and your descendants.*"

Gehazi had to leave the house, the town, and his family and live in the wilderness because of that awful disease.

LIFE APPLICATION

■ ■

{Ask:}

- Does God take sin seriously? [*Yes*]

- Have you ever heard a person say, *"God never gives us more than we can handle?"* [*Allow answers.*]

This saying is false. God always gives us more than we can handle because He wants us to totally rely upon Him and not ourselves.

{Hold up the poster. Read it aloud.}

The Scripture on the poster tells us that God will not allow for you to be TEMPTED beyond what you can handle.

{Ask:}

- Think of Gehazi. What should he have done when Naaman left? [*Go back to what he was doing and not run after him*]

- What could Gehazi have done when he stopped for a breath while running after Naaman? [*Turned around and gone back home*]

- What could Gehazi have done when he caught up with Naaman? [*Said, "I am sorry. I made a mistake," and gone back home*]

- What could Gehazi have done when Naaman gave him the money and clothes? [*Given them back and gone home*]

- What could Gehazi have done when the servants turned to walk back to their master? [*Given the stuff back*]

- What could Gehazi have done instead of hiding the treasure? [*Given it to Elisha and confessed*]

- What could Gehazi have done instead of lying to Elisha? [*Confessed what he did*]

- Did God give Gehazi ways of escape throughout this experience? [*Yes!*]

Gehazi did not choose any of those options and was given leprosy as a consequence.

God will ALWAYS give you a way to escape temptation. He will not allow more temptation than you can handle. You can never say that you had no choice but to sin. God always asks us to do hard things that we cannot do in our own power. When you are being tempted, you need to start talking to God, asking Him to open your eyes to see the way of escape.

It will be there.

What can we learn from Gehazi? If we want to be godly, we must remember that God wants us to rely upon Him and to trust that He will provide an escape when we are being tempted to sin.

COMMENT BOX

■ ■

THINK: What went well as you taught this lesson? What can you do better?

_____

_____

_____

_____

_____

_____

_____

_____

_____

_____

TIP: It is possible for this lesson to have great interaction between you and the children. As an extension, have the kids come up with "ways of escape" from different temptations such as lying, stealing from a friend, boasting about awards won, breaking something that belongs to someone else, etc.

7 HOW SNEAKY IS MANIPULATION?

■ ■

Have you ever tried to do "just enough" to meet a requirement? What about trying to get around a rule? This object lesson about Ananias and Sapphira will help our children understand that lying, manipulation, and general sneakiness are not steps in the right direction on the narrow path of godliness. {Deuteronomy 5:32}

Scripture Focus: Acts 5:1-11

Materials:

- Baking pan

- Aluminum foil

- Many brown *E*'s cut out of brown construction paper

- Consider making real brownies to give out at the end of the lesson

- Proverbs 15:3 poster

FUTUREFLYINGSAUCERS.COM

The eyes of the Lord are in every place, keeping watch on the evil and the good.

—Proverbs 15:3 (NASB)

OBJECT LESSON

■ ■

{Before class, place the *E*'s in the pan and put aluminum foil over it. Act VERY excited, but do not lie! Be sure to pronounce "brown *E*'s" as "brownies."}

This pan is full of brown *E*'s!! I cooked this afternoon, and out of the goodness of my heart, I brought in brown E's for all of you!! The kitchen smelled so good!! Would you like to have one? [*Kids should be excited and ready for a yummy brownie.*]

{If possible, be in the middle of the group. Carefully peel away the top and begin handing out the "brown *E*'s." Allow the children to react to your trick.}

{Ask:}

- What? Why are you disappointed and upset? [*Accept answers. Create a list of feelings the children had when they realized it was a trick. Be careful! The kids became quite angry with me when they saw that I had tricked them!!*]

- Did I have to bring you brownies today? [*No*]

- My bringing you brownies would have been a treat—a blessing, a gift. Instead, what did you receive? [*Nothing, a trick*]

BIBLE LESSON

■ ■■ ■

Jesus had come, died, risen, and ascended into heaven. The Holy Spirit had been given to the disciples with the sound of a great wind. The early church was growing every day. Some of the people decided to sell certain objects and properties and bring all of the money to Peter and the disciples so it could be used to help anyone in need.

For some reason, Ananias and his wife, Sapphira, sold a piece of property. They kept a portion of the profit for themselves and then planned to give the remainder to the apostles. There is nothing wrong with doing that.

The problem comes from what Ananias and Sapphira planned. They planned to make themselves look better than they really were. They decided to be sneaky and trick the apostles into thinking they were giving the ENTIRE amount of money from selling the land instead of only a portion.

However, God knows everything, and Peter had a discerning Spirit within him. When Ananias brought the money to Peter, he confronted him and asked, *"Ananias, why has Satan filled your heart to lie to the Holy Spirit?"*

The land money was theirs. They could do what they wanted with it. However, bringing a portion and lying about the amount was lying to God.

Ananias had no time to respond. He fell to the ground, took his last breath, and died. Men picked up his body and buried him.

Three hours later, Sapphira came to Peter, not knowing what had happened. Peter asked her if the amount stated by Ananias was the whole amount for the property. She agreed with her husband's number.

Peter responded, *"How is it you two planned together to test the Spirit? The men who buried your husband are here to bury you."* Then she fell to the ground, took a last breath, and died.

The young men came into the room, picked her up, and buried her next to her husband.

LIFE APPLICATION

■ ■ ■ ■ ■ ■ ■ ■ ■ ■ ■ ■ ■ ■ ■ ■ ■ ■ ■ ■

{Ask:}

- Did I HAVE to bring you brownies today? [*No*]

- Did Ananias and Sapphira HAVE to give all of their money to the church? [*No*]

Their sneakiness, or trickiness, is seen when they try to keep some of the money and then lie about the amount given to Peter. They were trying to look generous while being greedy.

Sometimes when we try to trick people, we bring others in on our "joke." Ananias could have lied on his own. Instead, his wife was a part of the trick as well.

{Ask:}

- Why do we not die when we lie? [*Allow for answers.*]

- What do all people deserve? [*The wages of sin is death.*]

The fact that we do not die when we sin is grace and mercy from God. God could take our lives if He wanted to. For some reason He chose to do this with Ananias and Sapphira. They became an example to the early church.

God takes sin seriously. We should as well.

{Hold up the poster. Read it aloud.}

{Ask:}

- Where are the eyes of the Lord? [*In every place*]

- If you are in your bedroom by yourself, or outside by yourself, are you ever alone? [*No*] No, God is always with you. He will never leave you. He will not abandon you.

- What does God watch over? [*The evil and the good*] God sees everything you do—the good and the bad, good choices and bad choices. He sees your heart.

- What should we do when we begin to think about tricking someone? What should we do when we begin to think about saying something about another person? What should we do when we begin to think about trying to do something we know is wrong when we are by ourselves? [*Allow for answers.*]

The Bible tells us to take every thought captive. (2 Corinthians 10:5) When we begin to start thinking negative thoughts about a person or situation, we need to tell ourselves, "*No! Stop thinking that! God wants me to be honest. He wants me to be pure. He wants me to honor Him all the time.*"

What can we learn from Ananias and Sapphira? If we want to be godly, we must remember that God knows our thoughts and motivations, and that He cannot be tricked.

COMMENT BOX

■ ■

THINK: What went well as you taught this lesson? What can you do better?

_____

_____

_____

_____

_____

_____

_____

_____

_____

_____

_____

TIP: Even though you are a Bible teacher, you will sin. When you do, if applicable, share your failure with your students. When we become a picture of redemption, children will begin to see *why* humanity needs a Savior.

8 HOW IS YOUR SELF-CONTROL?

■ ■ ■ ■ ■ ■ ■ ■ ■ ■ ■ ■ ■ ■ ■ ■ ■ ■ ■

We live in a world where everyone does what is right in his or her own eyes. Self-control is not a valued character trait. Here is a fun self-control object lesson that kids can do themselves. Helping our children understand the importance of self-control is a step in the right direction on the narrow path of godliness. {Deuteronomy 5:32}

Scripture Focus: Joshua 7

Materials:

- A wide mouth jar without a top, or a cup

- A tennis ball

- A plastic bowl

- A toilet paper roll

- Proverbs 25:28 poster

Make sure the ball fits into the jar. I used a cheese dip jar. If you feel daring, use a raw egg instead of the ball!

Like a city that is broken into and without walls is a man who has no control over his spirit.

—Proverbs 25:28 (NASB)

FUTUREFLYINGSAUCERS.COM

OBJECT LESSON

■ ■ ■ ■ ■ ■ ■ ■ ■ ■ ■ ■ ■ ■ ■ ■ ■ ■ ■ ■

{Place the jar right-side up on a table. Center the bowl on top of the jar. Stand the toilet paper roll in the middle of the bowl. Place the tennis ball on top of the roll. This is a physics experiment for teaching laws of motion, but we're going to use it for self-control. Be sure to practice the experiment and adjust the placement of the toilet paper roll, if needed.}

Let's predict.

{Ask:}

• What do you think will happen if I knock the bowl out of the way? [*Allow for answers.*]

Let's see who is correct. First I am going to try to hit the bowl with a little bit of force.

{With your hand about 12 inches from the bowl, slowly and lightly move your hand to strike the bowl to the left (or right). The bowl should not move much. The ball might fall off, but it is not much fun to watch.}

{Ask:}

• What happened? [*Allow answers.*]

• What do you think would happen if I knocked the bowl REALLY, REALLY hard? [*Everything would go flying across the room.*]

{Allow the children to imagine, or you can actually hit it hard. Be careful to not hit any children with the materials.}

Hitting the bowl with too little or too much force will cause our experiment to not work correctly. I must knock the bowl with just the right amount of force. **{Knock the bowl out and the tennis ball should fall right into the jar.}**

BIBLE LESSON

God used Joshua and the Israelites to destroy Jericho. One of the requirements God gave to Joshua was that none of the Israelites were to take anything from Jericho.

The next city to conquer was Ai. Joshua sent spies to the surrounding area, and they were to report back to him. The report concluded that the city had few people and that only 2,000 to 3,000 soldiers were needed to destroy it.

Joshua sent 3,000 men to fight. What was supposed to be an easy battle ended up with the Israelites retreating and 36 men dead.

Joshua, totally confused, fell on his face before the Lord. God then told him that Israel had sinned. He told Joshua that someone had taken some of the riches from Jericho. God explained to Joshua that he needed to find the man and get rid of him.

Joshua called all of Israel to come before him. By casting lots, or using dice, he figured out that the man came from the tribe of Judah. By process of elimination, Achan stood before Joshua. Joshua told him, "*Glorify God and confess what you have done.*"

Achan replied that when he saw the spoils of Jericho, he coveted them. With a lack of self-control, he gathered up some of the riches and buried them beneath his tent.

Joshua sent messengers to go to Achan's tent to find the spoils. They brought them back and laid them before the Lord.

Joshua took Achan, all of the spoils from Jericho, all of his animals, his tent, and his sons and daughters outside the camp. The Israelites then stoned them to death and burned everything with fire.

LIFE APPLICATION

■ ■

When we think about this event, we must remember that God is a holy God. We must also remember the verse that states, *"The wages of sin is death."* (Romans 6:23)

{Ask:}

- What did Achan say caused him to take the spoils of Jericho? [*He coveted them.*]

Coveting means wanting something that does not belong to you. Coveting is sin. That is one of the Ten Commandments. Then Achan went even farther and broke another commandment: stealing. He did not control himself. Coveting was bad enough...but then he acted on that sin that was in his heart.

- What is self-control? [*Allow for answers. Self-control is the ability to control one's emotions and actions.*]

{Set up the experiment again.} Sometimes we are like this experiment. **{Hit the bowl lightly.}** There are times when we do not control ourselves and we are lazy. We do not put much effort into doing something. Perhaps it is school work, or trying to do better at a sport, or reading our Bibles.

{Pretend to hit the bowl REALLY hard.} Pretend I hit this too hard. Sometimes we overindulge. Maybe you talk too much, eat too much food, or act too crazy in the classroom. These are examples of a lack of self-control. This experiment does not work well with the wrong amount of force.

{Ask:}

- What is the fruit of the Spirit? [*See if they can list all nine: love, joy, peace, patience, kindness, goodness, faithfulness, gentleness, and self-control.*]

Self-control comes to us from the Holy Spirit. We must ask Him for help with our self-control. **{Do the experiment again with the ball landing in the jar.}** We cannot have good self-control without the Holy Spirit. We receive the Holy Spirit when we ask Jesus to save us from our sins. Our lives will only work right when we have the Holy Spirit guiding us.

{Hold up the poster. Read it aloud.}

Think about the city of Ai. It did not have strong walls like Jericho. It did not have many people living in it, either. Ai should have been easily destroyed. That is what a person is like without self-control. You are like a city that can be easily destroyed.

{Ask:}

- What will destroy you? What destroyed Achan? [*Sin*] Sin will destroy you. Bad choices will destroy you.

- Who else was destroyed by Achan's decision to lack self-control? [*His family*] When we make poor decisions and show a lack of self-control, we can destroy ourselves and our families.

- What are some ways you lose your self-control? [*Allow for answers: anger, laziness, manipulation, greediness, gluttony, etc.*]

Those of us who have Jesus as our Lord and Savior have a strong wall that surrounds us. The Father, the Son, and the Holy Spirit surround us. We are safe from the enemy when we obey God. However, when we decide to step outside the wall and do our own thing, we are defenseless and our poor decisions will hurt us and those we love.

What can we learn from Achan? If we want to be godly, we must ask the Holy Spirit every day to give us the fruit of the Spirit, which includes self-control.

COMMENT BOX

■ ■

THINK: What went well as you taught this lesson? What can you do better?

_____

_____

_____

_____

_____

_____

_____

_____

_____

_____

_____

TIP: If you teach a Bible lesson that is interesting, engaging, and applicable, children will begin to learn that Jesus is interesting, engaging, and applicable to their lives.

9 RESPECTING THE RIGHTS OF OTHERS

■ ■

Everyone seems to be focused on their personal rights these days—the right to say what we want; the right to do what we want; the right to bear arms; the right to life; the right to have an education. According to the Bible, what are our rights? Helping our children understand the importance of respecting the rights of others is a step in the right direction on the narrow path of godliness. {Deuteronomy 5:32}

Scripture Focus: Genesis 13

Materials:

- Collect pairs of three types of items; have one of each pair be new and the other used or worthless.

- Galatians 5:14 poster

I used a new pair of socks and an old pair of socks, one new pencil and one sharpened and chewed pencil, and one whole cookie and one cookie with a bite out of it.

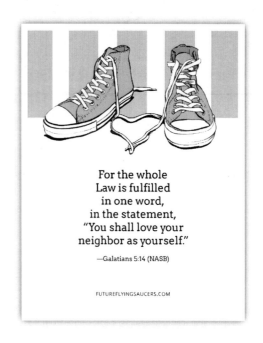

For the whole
Law is fulfilled
in one word,
in the statement,
"You shall love your
neighbor as yourself."

—Galatians 5:14 (NASB)

FUTUREFLYINGSAUCERS.COM

OBJECT LESSON

■ ■ ■ ■ ■ ■ ■ ■ ■ ■ ■ ■ ■ ■ ■ ■ ■ ■ ■ ■

{Have all of your items in a bag so the children cannot see them. Choose one child to help you. Be sure to choose a child who is a good sport, has a personality that can handle silliness, and is respectful. Change the following dialogue to fit your objects.}

{Say to the child:} There are some items in this bag that I want to share with you. **{Pull out the two pencils.}** I really like pencils. Some can be so neat with pretty colors! I want to share a pencil with you. **{Aloud, go through the decision process for giving away the pencil.}** Which pencil should I give you? I really like this one. It has not been sharpened yet. It has a new eraser. This other pencil has been used and sharpened. It even has something sticky on it. There is no eraser. Hmm...I think I will keep the nice pencil. You can have the one that is already sharpened. **{Give the child the used pencil.}**

{Pull out the pairs of socks.} I have some socks to share! This pair is new and has never been worn. This pair is kind of grungy. **{Smell the socks.}** They are clean, but they look dirty. You know what? Both pairs of socks will keep feet warm and that is the point for wearing socks, so you can have this old pair, and I will keep the soft new pair. **{Give the child the old socks.}**

{By this time, the child (and probably many others!) will be disgusted with you for giving away the older items. Act as if you do not understand and continue with the final item.}

{Pull out one whole cookie and one broken cookie (or with a bite taken out of it.)} Ooooh! I love cookies! I will share a cookie with you! Um...**{Look at both cookies as if this is a difficult decision and then give the broken cookie to the child.}** Here. You probably do not like these cookies as much as I do, so you can have the broken one.

{The kids will probably be rowdy. Calm them down by asking these questions. Accept answers. Hopefully the children will recognize that even though sharing occurred, it was selfishly done.}

Why are you so upset? What is the big deal? I gave away a perfectly good pencil, some socks, and a cookie.

Did I deserve to keep the nicer items? Did the other person deserve to have the nicer items? How do we make decisions figuring out "who gets what"?

BIBLE LESSON

■ ■ ■ ■ ■ ■ ■ ■ ■ ■ ■ ■ ■ ■ ■ ■ ■ ■ ■ ■

Abraham had a similar situation, although what needed to be shared was much larger. Abraham and his family were following God and living as nomads in the land. That means they lived in tents and traveled around the land to feed their flocks.

Abraham was very rich. His nephew, Lot, who was traveling with him, was rich, too. The land was unable to supply the food and water that was needed for all of the animals. The herdsmen were fighting among themselves.

Abraham explained to Lot that he did not want strife, or trouble, between them. They were family. Therefore, Abraham showed the land to Lot. He told Lot that if he chose to go left, Abraham would go right, and vice versa.

Lot looked at all of the land. One part was a plain that was lush and green. The other part was more brown and rocky. Lot chose the better-looking land. He and his family went to live among the cities on the Jordan plain, and Abraham went the other way and dwelt in Canaan.

{Ask:}

- Who chose the nicer-looking land? [*Lot*]

Yes, and eventually Lot had problems. Genesis 14:12-16 tells us that the king of the city of Sodom captured Lot, and Abraham had to go and rescue him. Then in Genesis 19, the cities of Sodom and Gomorrah were so evil that the Lord destroyed them. Lot's wife disobeyed God and ended up turning into a pillar of salt. Sometimes the nicest-looking decision is not the best decision.

LIFE APPLICATION

■ ■ ■ ■ ■ ■ ■ ■ ■ ■ ■ ■ ■ ■ ■ ■ ■ ■

{Ask:}

- When given the decision to choose the land, could Abraham have said, "Lot, I am in charge. I am your uncle. I get to choose first"? [*Yes*]

But he did not. Abraham had the right to choose first. Instead, he allowed Lot to choose first, AND he allowed Lot to choose the better land. Abraham took the less desirable land, and eventually he was rewarded for his selfless decision. Abraham put his rights aside and let someone else go first.

{Hold up the poster. Read it aloud.}

{Ask:}

- Who is our neighbor? [*Everyone*]

- How are we to treat other people? [*Love them as we love ourselves*] Let's figure out what that means.

- Who has sinned? [*All have sinned. (Romans 3:23)*]

- What do all sinners deserve? [*Death (Romans 6:23)*]

- If you are a sinner and I am a sinner, and we all are sinners and deserve death, what rights do we have? [*The children might not know how to answer this question. The answer is: We have no rights.*]

People believe they have certain rights. They believe they deserve to do certain actions.

If there is anything good in us, it comes from God because of our faith in Him. (Philippians 3:9) You know those birthday presents you like to receive? You do not deserve them. You know that house you live in? You do not deserve to live there. You know those parents and family members you have? You do not deserve them.

Everything you have comes from God. All of those presents, your home, and your family members are wonderful blessings that God has chosen to give to you. He gives them to you because He loves you, and not because you deserve them.

We think we deserve to have the best all the time.

We want what is best all the time. To love our neighbors as ourselves means that, instead of us keeping what is best, we give it away. We don't give away the best things because the other person deserves it. We give away the best things because we are to love that person as Jesus loves us. Whether it is a toy, a pencil, the best place in line, a pair of socks, or an argument we want to win, loving our neighbor means choosing to be like Abraham—choosing to be like Jesus.

Jesus died on the cross while we were still sinners. We do not deserve salvation. It is a gift. God gave His only Son as a sacrifice for all of our selfish thoughts and actions. Jesus died, took all of our sins upon Himself, and rose again. Therefore, we can choose to have eternal life with God in heaven. Jesus put His rights aside so that we could choose eternal life instead of death.

Strength comes from placing your rights to the side and allowing someone else to choose the better option.

What can we learn from Abraham and Lot? If we want to be godly, we must love others more than we love ourselves.

COMMENT BOX

■ ■ ■ ■ ■ ■ ■ ■ ■ ■ ■ ■ ■ ■ ■ ■ ■ ■ ■ ■

THINK: What went well as you taught this lesson? What can you do better?

_____

_____

_____

_____

_____

_____

_____

_____

_____

_____

TIP: Be sure to bring spare cookies if your helper eats the broken one you give away. Plus, it might be fun to give all of the kids a cookie when the lesson is over!

10 WHEN IS IT OKAY TO DISOBEY AUTHORITY?

■ ■ ■ ■ ■ ■ ■ ■ ■ ■ ■ ■ ■ ■ ■ ■ ■

Respecting authority is important. It helps us to be good citizens. However, when is it okay to disobey authority? Looking at events in the lives of Jesus, Paul, the disciples, and some midwives will help our children understand God's authority versus man's authority. This is a step in the right direction on the narrow path of godliness. {Deuteronomy 5:32}

Scripture Focus: Matthew 22:15-22; Acts 16:37; Exodus 1:18-22; Acts 5:27-42

Materials:

- Your nation's flag

- Deuteronomy 12:32 poster

Background: When God gave Moses and the Israelites the Law, it was understood that God would lead and the people would follow. Israel was to be a different nation led by a living God. However, the people looked around and saw that other nations had a king, a leader who was human.

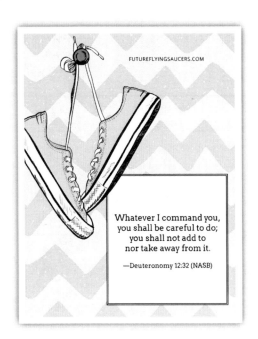

FUTUREFLYINGSAUCERS.COM

Whatever I command you,
you shall be careful to do;
you shall not add to
nor take away from it.

—Deuteronomy 12:32 (NASB)

Eventually God led Samuel to choose a king and then Israel was "like the other nations." God warned the people that having a king would mean they would lose certain freedoms.

OBJECT LESSON

{Hold up the flag.}

{Ask:}

- What do you think of when you see this flag? [*Allow for answers. Lead them to be patriotic in nature. I found that younger kids needed more help with this question.*]

{If you live in a country other than the United States, change the wording of this lesson to match your country.}

We (the people of the United States) live in a nation that is a federal republic. We elect people to represent us in Washington, DC. Those representatives are elected to represent the thoughts, cares, and beliefs of the people of their state when they create and pass laws.

Sometimes we like the laws they pass, and sometimes we disagree with them. However, when a law is passed, we must obey the law. We can try to get the law changed, but we must obey the law.

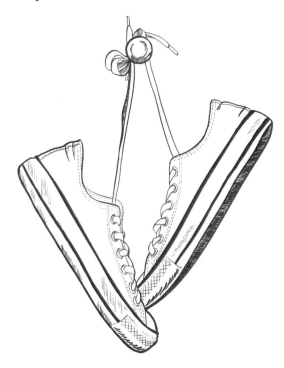

BIBLE LESSON

{Show the flag again.}

{Ask:}

- What does it mean to be a good citizen? [*Allow answers*.]

Being a good citizen means:

1. **You know and obey the laws.** Many of us know *some* laws, but there are laws we know nothing about. During the political process of choosing a president, there are many laws and issues talked about of which many people are ignorant. The Apostle Paul shows us in Acts 16 how important it is to know the laws of one's nation. He, a Roman citizen, had been accused, beaten, and put in jail. That was against Roman law. If he had not known that, then those who were in authority over him would have gotten away with treating him unfairly.

2. **You pay your taxes.** Every year we have to pay our taxes. Some people try not to do this. It is called tax evasion. It is illegal. People who are caught not paying their taxes might go to jail or be fined. The Pharisees tried to trick Jesus and asked him if it was lawful to pay taxes to Caesar, because the Jews hated paying taxes to Rome. Jesus knew what they were doing and asked for a coin. When they brought it to Him, He said, "*Give to Caesar what is Caesar's. Give to God what is God's.*"

3. **You vote.** Not everyone can go to the capital and express their opinion about everything. Therefore, communities will vote for people to lead them and represent them. People will attempt to choose a person who reflects what they believe and care about. It is important that we are educated about the people who want to be elected. The person with the most votes wins. What happens if someone is voted in and we do not agree with them? When it is time to vote again, we vote the person out.

There are a few other characteristics that make a good citizen, such as caring for people in the community. However, for the most part, a good citizen obeys the authority of his or her government. **Respecting authority is important.** It helps life move smoothly. It helps people get along with each other. Disputes are taken care of in a peaceful manner.

Children are to be good sons and daughters by respecting their parents. We are to all be good students by listening to and respecting the advice of elders.

Is it okay to disobey authority?

Exodus 1 tells us that a Pharaoh came to the throne who did not know Joseph. Remember, Joseph had brought his family to live in Egypt during the famine. During that time, the Israelites multiplied. The group was growing so fast and large that this new Pharaoh began to fear them, thinking they might rebel and overtake Egypt. He turned the Israelites into slaves. He told the midwives to allow baby girls to be born, but if a baby boy was born, they were to kill the baby.

However, the midwives feared God more than Pharaoh. They knew it was wrong to kill, and they disobeyed Pharaoh and allowed the boys to live. Eventually Pharaoh had all the baby boys thrown into the river. However, one boy was saved.

{Ask:}

- Do you know who that one boy was? [*Moses!*]

Acts chapter 5 tells us that the disciples were preaching in the Temple. They were arrested and put into prison. An angel released them and they went back to preaching in the temple, totally confusing the leadership.

They were again brought before the counsel. The high priest asked, *"Did we not strictly tell you to stop teaching in this name?"* (They were preaching in Jesus' name.)

Peter and the other apostles stated, *"We ought to obey God rather than men."*

LIFE APPLICATION

■ ■ ■ ■ ■ ■ ■ ■ ■ ■ ■ ■ ■ ■ ■ ■ ■ ■ ■

{Hold up the poster. Read it aloud.}

{Ask:}

- How do we know what God commands? [*By reading the Bible*] God is the ultimate authority. His words and ways win, no matter what.

- Think about those midwives. Was Pharaoh asking them to do something that went against God's words and ways? [*Yes. He wanted them to kill the babies.*]

- Whom did the midwives obey? [*God*] Yes, and God rewarded them.

- Think about the disciples. The Temple leaders did not want them to preach in Jesus' name. But what were the last directions Jesus gave to his followers before he ascended? [*To be His witnesses and tell people of all nations about Him (Mark 16:15; Acts 1:8)*]

- Were the leaders going against God? [*Yes*]

- Whom did the disciples obey? [*Jesus; Holy Spirit*]

Words do not express how important it is to know God's laws and His ways. If someone asks you to do something, you need to know if it is okay with God or not. If it reflects God, everything is fine. If it does not reflect God, you have to decide whom you will obey. The midwives and the disciples understood that they could get in trouble with authorities if they disobeyed. They knew they could lose their lives, but they feared God more.

Some situations are easy to figure out. Do not steal. Do not murder someone. But what if an adult wants you to do something you know is wrong? What if that adult wants to touch you in an inappropriate way, or hits you? What if an employer wants you to lie about some money? What if a teacher will not allow you to write about or talk about Jesus? Do you respect his or her authority?

Are you going to obey God, or are you going to obey people?

Biblically, an adult does not have permission to treat you in a harmful, angry manner. Will parents discipline? Yes, that is their job. However, if any adult attempts to harm a child in any way, such as punch or injure, say really hateful words, or touch inappropriately, that adult is not an authority that is to be respected. If something like that happens to you or one of your friends, go tell what happened to an adult you trust immediately.

What can we learn from Jesus, Paul, and the midwives? If we want to be godly, we must respect our government, our parents, and other authorities. Only when asked to do something against God's commands do we choose God over man.

COMMENT BOX

■ ■

THINK: What went well as you taught this lesson? What can you do better?

_____

_____

_____

_____

_____

_____

_____

_____

_____

TIP: It is appropriate for teachers in the church to help children to know what steps to take if they find themselves in an abusive situation. The church should be seen as a safe place. Unfortunately, that is not always the case. Be sure that you take precautions to never be alone with a child. If you are in that situation, keep the door open so people can see you, or immediately go to a place where there are more people.

11 DEALING WITH REBELLION

■ ■

Rebellion. Is it really that bad of a thing? Helping our children understand why rebellion is harmful is a step in the right direction on the narrow path of godliness. {Deuteronomy 5:32}

Scripture Focus: Numbers 21:4-9; John 3:14

Materials:

- Print out pictures of the Star of Life, the Rod of Asclepius, and of a caduceus from the Resources Page. (Be sure to label them so there is no confusion.)

- 1 Samuel 15:23 poster

Background: The Israelites have been wandering in the desert. Many years have gone by. Moses hit the rock for water instead of speaking to it. Aaron died. The forty years are almost completed.

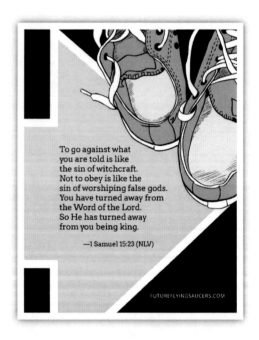

To go against what you are told is like the sin of witchcraft. Not to obey is like the sin of worshiping false gods. You have turned away from the Word of the Lord. So He has turned away from you being king.

—1 Samuel 15:23 (NLV)

FUTUREFLYINGSAUCERS.COM

OBJECT LESSON

{Hold up the picture of the caduceus.}

{Ask:}

- Where have you seen this symbol before? [*On ambulances, at doctors' offices, on uniforms, hospitals*]

- Are you sure it is this symbol? [*Yes*]

- Or is it this symbol?

{Hold up the picture of the Star of Life. The children should be confused, but they should recognize the similarities of the two symbols.}

Those in the United States are sometimes confused and use these symbols interchangeably. But they are different and represent two different ideas.

{Hold up the picture of the caduceus.}

This symbol is called a caduceus. It was used in Greek mythology. The stories talk about how the staff of the god Hermes could put people to sleep or wake them up.

{Hold up the picture of the Rod of Asclepius.}

Asclepius was also a Greek god who had a rod. He was in charge of all health and medicine. In 1902, the United States Army made an error and put the caduceus on their medical uniforms instead of what is called the Rod of Asclepius. It makes more sense to use the rod for health and medicine on medical uniforms instead of a rod that makes people sleep or wake up.

{Hold up the picture of the Star of Life.}

This is what we should see on any type of medical building, transportation, or health uniform. This is called the Star of Life. This was designed for the Emergency Medical Service. If you see something that is supposed to represent medicine and the symbol has wings on it, then you know they have the symbol wrong.

{Ask:}

- Where have you seen this symbol? [*Paramedic uniforms, nurse uniforms, hospitals, doctors' offices, etc.*]

BIBLE LESSON

■ ■ ■ ■ ■ ■ ■ ■ ■ ■ ■ ■ ■ ■ ■ ■ ■ ■ ■ ■

Historians say that these symbols came from the Greeks, and maybe from people even before the Greek Empire. However, we know that the symbol comes from God in the Old Testament.

The Israelites had been in the desert for years. We are told in Numbers chapter 20 that Aaron, Moses' brother, had died. Israel had just defeated the Canaanites, and they traveled on. The people became discouraged in their souls, and they began to grumble against Moses and God.

The people rebelled by saying, *"Why have you brought us this way? There is no food or water, and our souls* **hate** *this manna!!"* Wow! Manna was the food God had been providing for them to eat.

Because of their rebellion and complaining, God sent poisonous snakes into the camp. The snakes would bite the people, and the people would die. Eventually, the people of Israel went to Moses and repented. They said, *"We have sinned against God and you. Please pray to the Lord and ask Him to take away the serpents."*

Moses did pray, but God did not take away the serpents. Instead, he told Moses to make a bronze snake and put it on a pole. Moses then told the people that if they were bitten, they were to look at the snake on the pole and they would be healed.

LIFE APPLICATION

{Ask:}

- What would happen if the people chose to not look at the serpent on the pole? [*They would die.*] Rebellion, or to rebel, is defined as "to refuse obedience."

- **{Hold up the Star of Life.}** Why do people use this symbol? What does it represent? [*Good health, healing, life*]

- Would it be fair to say that disobedience or rebellion can bring death, and obedience can bring life? [*Accept answers.*]

{Hold up the poster. Read it aloud.}

This verse was told to Saul after he had rebelled against God. Saul had rebelled against God, so God then turned away His blessings from Saul. Saul eventually died and lost the kingdom.

If an Israelite girl or boy was bitten by a snake, all they had to do was obey **God's words** and look at the serpent on the pole, and they would be healed. But if they rebelled and did not look at the serpent, they would die.

God takes rebellion seriously. Samuel, God's prophet, who said the verse on the poster, tells us that rebellion is just as bad as witchcraft and worshiping false gods. People want life and healing. **{Show the Star of Life.}**

{Ask:}

- If a person is sick and the doctor gives a specific medicine that will help that person, what should that person do? [*Take the medicine.*]

- What if the person decides not to take the medicine? [*That person might stay sick longer or not heal well.*]

LIFE and HEALING is in OBEDIENCE. However, sometimes people do not want to obey. Instead, they rebel.

For example, a person has a heart attack and the doctor says, *"You need to eat healthy food and exercise."* However, that person continues to eat junk food and does not exercise.

{Ask:}

- What do you think might happen to that person? [*He might have another heart attack and die.*] Rebellion brings about death.

- Do you ever rebel? [*Allow for answers*.] Rebellion is disobedience and both are examples of sin. We are all sinners.

- What is the consequence for sin? [*Death*]

Jesus had a conversation with a man named Nicodemus. Jesus said that just as Moses lifted the serpent in the desert, so will the Son of Man be lifted up; those who believe will have eternal life.

{Ask:}

- What happens to people who believe in Jesus? [*They will have eternal life.*]

- What happens to those who do not believe? Will they have eternal life? [*No*] That is what happened with the Israelites. If they looked at the serpent, they lived. If they did not, they died.

This Scripture on the poster tells us what to do: **Do not turn away from the Word of the Lord**. God took the kingdom away from Saul because of his rebelliousness. He missed out on wonderful blessings.

You could miss out on God's blessings, too, if you disobey and rebel against God. The ultimate rebellion is to not believe in Jesus. That decision brings death.

{Ask:}

- Who are we to obey? [*God, parents, teachers...*] Yes. We are to obey those in authority. The only time we do not obey authority is when someone tries to harm us or get us to do something that goes against God and His ways.

What can we learn from Moses, the snakes, and God? If we want to be godly, we must choose to obey God and other authorities and not be rebellious. We don't want to miss God's blessings.

COMMENT BOX

■ ■ ■ ■ ■ ■ ■ ■ ■ ■ ■ ■ ■ ■ ■ ■ ■ ■ ■ ■

THINK: What went well as you taught this lesson? What can you do better?

_____

_____

_____

_____

_____

_____

_____

_____

_____

TIP: Many Bible teachers are concerned by students who reflect apathy toward the Bible and church. An important truth to teach is that God takes our sin seriously. If students understand their need for Jesus, learning how to please Him becomes a lifelong goal. If apathy is a concern for you, pray that the Holy Spirit would work in the hearts of your students, and then keep teaching them. There will be fruit one day.

12 HOW TO HANDLE BOASTING

Everyone likes to succeed. No one likes to look foolish in the eyes of others. This lesson will explore the familiar Bible story of David and Goliath and the boasting that led to destruction. Being able to handle success and failure will help our children take a step in the right direction on the narrow path of godliness. {Deuteronomy 5:32}

Scripture Focus: 1 Samuel 17

Materials:

- Tape measure

- 1 Corinthians 1:26-29 poster

Background: 1 Samuel 17 tells us that Goliath was about 6 cubits and a span tall. A cubit was around 18 inches (46 cm). This measurement would place Goliath around 9 feet (2.7 meters) tall. He was from the city of Gath, which was a powerful Philistine city.

The book of Samuel tells us what happened during the reign of King Saul, the first king of Israel. He did not have a whole heart for God. Therefore, God was setting up His plan for a new king. Not only did this plan include a new king of Israel, but it also included a King who would reign forever and ever.

OBJECT LESSON

■ ■ ■ ■ ■ ■ ■ ■ ■ ■ ■ ■ ■ ■ ■ ■ ■ ■ ■ ■

{Use the tape measure to show 6 feet (1.8 meters), the average height of a man. Then pull it out to 9 feet (2.7 meters). Discuss the difference. If you are in a room with a high ceiling, turn the tape measure vertical so the children can see how tall 9 feet (2.7 meters) is. My room was not tall enough, and the kids realized that Goliath's head would go through the ceiling tiles!}

{Ask:}

- What emotions would you feel if a man 9 feet (2.7 meters) tall entered this room? [*Allow answers*.]

- Would you want to be his friend or make him mad at you? [*Be his friend!*]

- Do any of you watch wrestling on TV? [*Allow answers*.] Those men strut around a ring claiming they are so great, and then they wrestle, or fight, each other to see who wins.

- What kind of boasting do you think a 9-feet-tall (2.7 meters-tall) wrestler might do? [*Allow answers.*]

BIBLE LESSON

Saul found himself at war with the Philistines. **{Have the kids "boo" the Philistines throughout the lesson.}** The Philistine army was on one mountain, and the Israelites were on the top of another mountain. The Valley of Elah was between them.

Goliath, THE Philistine champion, went into the valley and boasted to the Israelites, *"Send out your best soldier. If you win the battle, then all of us will serve you. But if I win, then you will serve the Philistines!"* Goliath continued to boast and brag and make fun of the Israelite army for 40 days.

David happened to visit his brothers who were in Saul's army while this was going on. *"Who is this unclean Philistine that he should treat God's army like that?"* he asked.

Once told, David decided that he should be the one to fight Goliath; after all, he had killed a lion and a bear while protecting sheep. Goliath could be no worse than those animals.

King Saul heard the rumor about David and called him to the king's tent. David assured Saul that he would fight Goliath and win. Saul offered his own armor to David, but after trying it on, David said he would use his own weapons.

Once again Goliath began to mock and boast against the army of the Lord, and David went out to meet him. Goliath said, *"Am I a dog that you send such a one out to fight me with sticks? I will feed your flesh to the birds!"*

David responded by running at Goliath, crying, *"You come to me with sword and shield, but I come to you in the name of the Lord of Hosts, the God of the armies of Israel whom you...have...defied!!"* **{Make sure you yell this quote while acting like you are "twirling" a sling shot. It is powerful!}**

Goliath was enraged and ran toward David. David slung a stone at the large man and hit him. After Goliath fell down dead, David cut off Goliath's head and took it to Saul.

LIFE APPLICATION

■ ■ ■ ■ ■ ■ ■ ■ ■ ■ ■ ■ ■ ■ ■ ■ ■ ■ ■ ■

{Hold up the poster. Read it aloud.}

{Ask:}

- In the eyes of those in the armies, who was wise? [*King Saul*]

- Who was powerful? [*Goliath*]

- Who was rich? [*King Saul*]

- Who was strong? [*Goliath*]

- Who seemed foolish? [*David*]

- Who brought shame to the wise? [*David*]

- Who brought shame to the strong? [*David*]

- Whom did God choose to help? [*David*]

- In whom did David boast? [*God*]

- What are some examples of boasting that you might hear today? [*Allow answers.*]

- Is it wrong to be proud of the good things we do? [*No*]

It is not bad for us to be successful. It is not wrong for us to be proud when we make good choices and do good things. However, we must always remember that it is GOD who gives us the ability to do everything we do. There is nothing good in us. God is the only one who is good.

David was proud of himself after the fight was over. But he knew who had given him the power to fight. David knew that without God, he could do nothing. David did not boast in what HE did, but in what he knew GOD could do and would do.

{Ask:}

- What are some ways that we can boast in God instead of ourselves? [*Allow answers.*]

{Ask:}

- What is the opposite of boasting? [*Being humble*]

- How can we act in a humble way? [*Put other people before yourself. Consider other people better than yourself. Allow others to tell of your good deeds.*]

What can we learn from David? If we want to be godly, we must choose to acknowledge that God is the one with all the power and boast in Him.

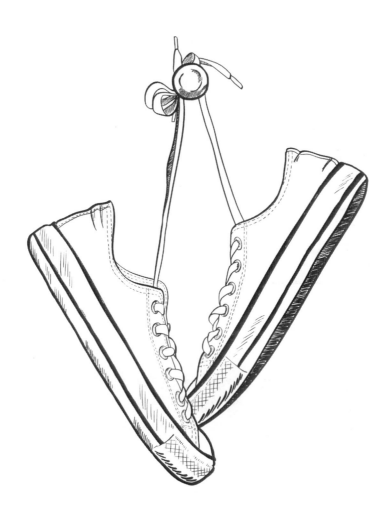

COMMENT BOX

■ ■

THINK: What went well as you taught this lesson? What can you do better?

_____

_____

_____

_____

_____

_____

_____

_____

_____

_____

TIP: When you teach, be sure to always have your Bible open to the Scripture you are teaching. Even if you do not read it to the students, you never know when a question might be asked. Always go back to the Scripture, and make sure your students read the Scripture as well.

13 GREEN WITH JEALOUSY AND ENVY

■ ■

It begins with a seed of discontent or a thought of insecurity. Jealousy is a green-eyed monster that must be slain. Helping our children understand why jealousy is harmful is a step in the right direction on the narrow path of godliness. {Deuteronomy 5:32}

Scripture Focus: 1 Samuel 18:6-16

Materials:

- A sheet of green paper

- 1 Corinthians 13:4 poster

Background: After David killed Goliath, he started to become famous among the Israelites. Saul added David to his court. David played the harp for Saul whenever asked. Saul's son Jonathan became David's best friend. David served Saul well and was given many leadership opportunities. Life was looking great for David.

FUTUREFLYINGSAUCERS.COM

Love is patient and kind. Love is not jealous, it does not brag, and it is not proud.

—1 Corinthians 13:4 (ICB)

OBJECT LESSON

{Hold up the green paper.}

{Ask:}

- What color is this? [*Green*]

- What emotion do you feel when you see this color? [*Allow for answers.*]

- Have you ever heard the saying "green with envy"? What does it mean? [*Someone is jealous of someone else.*]

People who know a lot about words and where they come from think that the term "green with envy" began with the Greeks. The Greeks believed that emotions came from the organs in your body. The liver produces bile, which is a yellow-green color. So when people became jealous, the Greeks thought it was because the liver was producing too much bile, causing their faces to turn slightly green.

An author named Shakespeare used the phrase "green-eyed monster" to personify jealousy.

{Quote this with theatrical emotion!}

Act 3 of *Othello*:

O! beware my lord, of Jealousy;

*It is the **green-ey'd monster** which doth mock*

The meat it feeds on.

{Ask:}

- Jealousy and envy are similar, but they are not the same thing. What does it mean for a person to be jealous? [*Allow answers. Lead them to a definition similar to "the fear of losing something of value, especially a relationship."*]

- What does it mean to be envious? [*Allow answers. Wanting or wishing for something that belongs to someone else, such as a better job or a possession.*]

Being jealous is like a person who says, *"I do not want to lose this."* Being envious is like a person who says, *"I want what he has."*

{It might be helpful to write the words *jealousy* and *envy* on a board, drawing simple pictures to illustrate the definitions. For *jealousy,* draw a person figure not wanting to let go of something. For *envy*, show a person figure with arms open, chasing after another person figure holding a present. Act out the definitions as well. For jealousy, wrap your arms around yourself. For envy, point to another person.}

Neither of these attitudes are glorifying to God. Being a jealous person or being an envious person can cause health issues and hurt relationships. You must deal with the sin causing these emotions.

BIBLE LESSON

■ ■

David was a great servant of King Saul's. King Saul's son, Jonathan, loved David like a brother. Jonathan gave David his own cloak, armor, sword, and bow. The Scripture says that David behaved wisely wherever he went and that he was accepted by all the people.

After Saul sent David to fight the Philistines, David was coming home. The people came out onto the streets. The women sang and danced, calling out, *"Saul has killed thousands, but David, ten thousands."* Saul heard this, and then jealousy and envy filled his heart.

{Ask:}

- What was he afraid to lose? [*His kingdom*]

- Why was he envious of David? [*The people liked David better than they did King Saul, and Saul wanted that popularity.*]

From that day forward, Saul was angry and suspicious of David.

Wherever David went, he behaved in a wise manner. Saul watched this and was afraid of David, because he knew the Lord was with David and not with him.

One day when David was playing the harp for Saul, the king grabbed a spear and threw it at David. David escaped from situations like this twice.

All the people loved David. The jealousy and envy of King Saul would eventually cause David to run for his life and spend years in the wilderness, running from a King who was "green with envy" and had no heart for God.

LIFE APPLICATION

■ ■ ■ ■ ■ ■ ■ ■ ■ ■ ■ ■ ■ ■ ■ ■ ■ ■ ■ ■

{Ask:}

- Is jealousy a bad thing? [*Kids will say, "Yes."*] The Bible says that God is a jealous God. (Exodus 34:14) Scripture plainly tells us that God is good and perfect. So jealousy must not always be a bad thing. Most of the time, in the Bible, we hear of God being jealous when He is telling the people to stop worshiping idols.

- Do you remember what the definition of jealousy is? [*"I do not want to lose something."*]

- What relationship does God NOT want to lose? [*His relationship with people*]

If God sees that there is something taking you away from His presence, He is jealous for you. God loves you! He wants to bless you. He wants to spend time with you. He wants to use you. However, if you are distracted by other things and not listening to God or spending time with Him, your relationship with God becomes damaged. God does not want that.

{Hold up the poster. Read it aloud.}

1 Corinthians 13 is filled with definitions of love. Here we read that love is not jealous.

{Ask:}

- Is this the good form or bad form of jealousy? [*In this verse, it is the bad form of jealousy.*]

In 2 Corinthians 11:2, Paul says that he is "jealous [for the people] with a godly jealousy." This means that Paul saw the people behaving in ways that did not honor God, and he was jealous for them to have a right relationship with Jesus.

We are not to be jealous and envious of other people in such a way that we break relationships with others. Nor are we to be mean and angry and act like King Saul. **We are to be jealous with a godly jealousy, desiring all people to know Jesus and walk with Him.** We are not to be jealous OF people, but we are to be jealous FOR people.

What can we learn from King Saul? If we want to be godly, we must choose to not be jealous because of selfish reasons, but because we want people to know Christ.

COMMENT BOX

■ ■

THINK: What went well as you taught this lesson? What can you do better?

_____

_____

_____

_____

_____

_____

_____

_____

TIP: Are you a Bible teacher who has been teaching for a number of years, but you fear you made mistakes in the past with your teaching? Or are you a new Christian who desires to teach a new-found love for Jesus to young people, but you fear you do not know enough to teach? Fear not! Keep walking in the ways of the Lord and ask Him to develop your knowledge and teaching skills.

14 BEING A BEST FRIEND

■ ■

Everyone has friends. Everyone wants to be a friend to others. But what does that look like in God's eyes? Using the story of David and Jonathan will help our children understand true friendship. This is a step in the right direction on the narrow path of godliness. {Deuteronomy 5:32}

Scripture Focus: 1 Samuel 20

Materials:

- Two magnets (one weak "toy" magnet and one strong magnet)

- A pack of sticky notes

- Something to stick the magnets onto, such as a white board, metal door, or a cookie sheet

- John 15:13 poster

Greater love has
no one than this,
that one lay down
his life for his friends.

—John 15:13 (NASB)

FUTUREFLYINGSAUCERS.COM

Background: David killed Goliath. Saul added David to his court. Saul's son, Jonathan, became David's best friend. Jonathan gave David his robe, armor, sword, and bow.

Jonathan and David made a covenant between them to solidify their friendship. David served Saul well and was given many leadership opportunities, but Saul became jealous of David and tried to kill him.

OBJECT LESSON

■ ■

{Hold up the two magnets.}

{Ask:}

- What can you tell me about magnets? [*Accept answers.*]

Magnets are neat because they stick to objects. **{Have the two magnets stick to each other.}** The magnetic field is interesting because if the magnets are one way, they stick to each other. However, if you turn one magnet around, they repel each other. Magnets are also stronger than gravity.

{Show how the magnets will not stick, no matter what you do.}

I wonder how strong these magnets are. Magnetic fields can go through objects. Let's take these sticky notes and see how many we can stack on top of each other until the magnetic field is too weak to hold the magnet to the board.

{Use the weak magnet first. Put a sticky note on the board then put the magnet on the note. It should stick. Have the children predict the number of sticky notes it will take until the magnet does not stick anymore. Then add the notes one at a time and test with the magnet, until the magnet will not stick. It took me five sticky notes for the weak magnet. Then have them predict for the strong magnet. Add the sticky notes one at a time, then five at a time. My magnet stuck through my entire stack of sticky notes!}

BIBLE LESSON

■ ■ ■ ■ ■ ■ ■ ■ ■ ■ ■ ■ ■ ■ ■ ■ ■ ■ ■ ■

Scripture tells us that a true friend is always loyal (Proverbs 17:17). David and Jonathan are a perfect picture of this. Before David killed Goliath, the Bible tells us that Samuel anointed David as the next king of Israel. After David killed Goliath, Jonathan basically adopted David into his family as a brother, and they became the best of friends. David would play the harp for King Saul. King Saul placed David in leadership positions.

Eventually the king became jealous and fearful of David and wanted to kill him. He threw a spear at David and told Jonathan and all of his servants that they should kill David. Jonathan warned David and spoke to the king on David's behalf, and the king relented.

Sometime later, King Saul attempted to kill David again by throwing a spear at him. David escaped, but he knew the king wanted him dead. There was no way he could stay around the king, so he fled. The king pursued David in order to kill him.

David somehow made it to Jonathan. David asked his friend why King Saul was after him and why he wanted him dead. Jonathan would not believe him, but David insisted that the king would not tell his son his intentions because of Jonathan's friendship with David.

Jonathan and David made a plan. Jonathan was going to tell the king that David was going to skip dinner to go be with his family. If the king was content with him being gone, then everything was fine and David was not in trouble with the king. However, if Jonathan told King Saul that David was visiting his family and the king became angry, they would know that the king wanted David dead.

David worried about Jonathan's safety. He feared that King Saul would turn on Jonathan as well. Jonathan and David made a covenant. In three days after Jonathan knew the answer about King Saul and David, he would shoot three arrows near a certain rock. If Jonathan told his servant boy that the arrows were near, then all was well with David. If Jonathan told the boy that the arrows were beyond, then David would know to flee for his life.

Dinner came and went. David was not at the table. Dinner came again the second night. King Saul asked Jonathan where David was. Once given the answer, King Saul flew into a rage and threw a spear at Jonathan. He told Jonathan that David would take the kingdom from him. Jonathan wanted to know what David had done to deserve death. Jonathan was very angry and saddened by his father.

The third day Jonathan shot his arrows and announced that they were beyond the boy. When the boy was sent away, David came to Jonathan out of hiding. They hugged and wept. Jonathan told him to go in peace and to remember their covenant before the Lord between them and their descendants forever.

LIFE APPLICATION

■ ■

Sometimes people can be like two magnets that will never stick to each other. They are not mean to each other. However, they do not have anything in common and do not really care to hang out with each other. These are people who are called "acquaintances."

People stick with good friends. Even then, though, people can have friends for a short time or friendships that last an entire lifetime.

Many times you will mess up and treat your good friends poorly, or you might be treated poorly by your friends. Sometimes you are like the weak magnet. Perhaps you get into an argument with a friend, or a friend wrongs you in some way. **{Put the sticky notes up again to show how the weak magnet does not stick.}** Your friendship is not strong. Neither of you apologize or ask for forgiveness.

{Ask:}

- What will happen to that friendship? [*It will disappear.*] **{Have the magnet slide off the sticky notes.}**

Jonathan and David were like the strong magnet. Even though Jonathan did not believe David, their friendship was tight. **{Make the sticky note stack thicker.}**

Once Jonathan knew the truth, he committed treason (went against the king) to save his innocent friend and let him flee to freedom. He was almost killed by his father because of his friendship with David. **{Put the strong magnet on the stack of sticky notes.}**

{Hold up the poster. Read it aloud.}

{Ask:}

- Do you think Jonathan would have died trying to save David? [*Yes!*]

You are like David. You need to be saved. You need to be saved from your sin. You cannot be with God the Father because of your sin. The wages of sin is death. But you have a Friend who laid down His life for you so you can be saved from sin.

Jesus died so that you can stand sinless before God. His friendship is the strongest one we will ever have.

{Ask:}

- Think about the friends you have. Do you want to have a weak magnet friendship or a strong magnet friendship? [*Accept answers. Hopefully they want to be a strong friend to others.*]

The most loyal friends tell their friends about Jesus. They tell the truth. They accept apologies. They ask forgiveness. They do not give up on each other. They walk the road of life with each other and with Jesus.

What can we learn from Jonathan and David? If we want to be godly, we must be good, loyal friends to others. Even though friends are great, Jesus is the closest and best friend we can ever have!

COMMENT BOX

■ ■

THINK: What went well as you taught this lesson? What can you do better?

_____

_____

_____

_____

_____

_____

_____

_____

_____

_____

TIP: Even the best-planned lessons and activities that should last the allotted time can be executed more quickly than expected. Always have more activities planned than you think you need. You can sing simple songs or play worship CDs to fill the time slot. Keep a list of games that need few to no props to play. If you have a solid backup plan, you will be ready when that sermon runs long!

15

WHY SHOULD WE FOLLOW DIRECTIONS?

■ ■

Words that explain an assignment are there for a reason. Step-by-step directions for building a bookcase are given for a specific purpose. Helping our children understand why following directions is important is a step in the right direction on the narrow path of godliness. {Deuteronomy 5:32}

Scripture Focus: Genesis 6-7

Materials:

- A white board, an easel, or a large sheet of paper

- 2-3 sheets of paper with one simple drawing on each one, such as a smile face, a star, or a simple design

- Proverbs 3:1-2 poster

My son, don't forget my teaching, but let your heart keep my commands; for they will bring you many days, a full life, and well-being.
—Proverbs 3:1-2 (HCSB)

FUTUREFLYINGSAUCERS.COM

Background: In the first few chapters of Genesis, genealogies are listed and interesting facts are given about different people.

However, the main thing we see is how sin has spread. The wickedness was great and God was searching across the land for a man who was righteous.

OBJECT LESSON

{Choose three volunteers. Have them form a line, front to back. Give the first person a crayon or marker and have them line up in front of the board or paper.}

These kids are going to practice following directions. **{Give the last person one of the pictures, allowing the rest of the kids in the class to see it. Do not let the first two people in line see the picture.}** The person standing on the end of the line will use a finger to draw the picture given to him on the back of the person in front of him. Then the next person will draw the picture on the back of the next person. Finally, the first person will draw the picture on the board. No talking allowed. Let's see if they can follow each other's directions!

{Allow the kids to do this. If time permits, let them rotate so each person in line has a chance to draw on the board.}

{Ask:}

- Was this an easy task? Why not? What would have made it easier? [*Hopefully they will notice that it is easier to get information from the original source (the paper), but that paying close attention to the person giving directions was important.*]

BIBLE LESSON

Noah was given directions. The directions came from God. He was the original source of the information, so Noah could trust Him.

{Read these verses from Genesis 6:5-9, 13-14, 17-20, 22. Read these verses from chapter 7:2, 5-6, 9.}

God gave Noah detailed instructions for building the ark. God even told Noah why He was making the ark. Verse 22 tells us that Noah did everything God told him to do.

{Ask:}

- What would have happened if Noah had not followed God's instructions? What if he had decided to use a different type of wood or had made the ark smaller or larger in size? [*Perhaps the ark would not have been as strong or would not have been large enough to hold all the animals.*]

{Read Genesis 6:15-16.}

God gave specific instructions, and Noah followed them without question.

{Ask:}

- What was Noah doing with God before he was asked to make the ark? [*Noah walked with God.*]

- Do you think Noah's walking with God would have made it easier or harder to follow God's directions? [*Easier*]

- Why? [*Allow for answers, but make sure they focus on relationship and trust.*]

LIFE APPLICATION

{Ask:}

- If God told you to build an ark, would you? [*Allow for answers.*]

- Has God ever given you directions? [*Allow for answers, but they might say no. If they say yes, ask them to tell you what God asked them to do.*]

God gives us many directions. He gave us the Bible, and it is filled with instructions for us to have a great life here on earth.

{Hold up the poster. Read it aloud.}

{Ask:}

- How do we not forget God's teachings? [*By regularly reading the Bible and memorizing Scripture.*]

- How do we let our hearts keep the commands? [*Allow for answers; lead them to consider that public obedience is great, but that most obedience comes from our attitudes and thoughts, which people never see.*]

- Are there rewards for following God's commands? [*Yes! Long life of many days, a full life, and well-being*]

- If we always obey God's directions, will we have nothing bad happen to us and will we live until we are 100 years old? [*No*] No, we will still have bad things happen to us because we live in a fallen world or because of sinful people. We will make bad choices because we are not perfect. Consider Jesus. He perfectly obeyed God's directions, and He died when He was about 33 years old. (See Luke 3:23.)

- If we are trying our hardest to follow God's directions, is it **less likely** or **more likely** that we will make good and healthy choices? [*More likely that we will make good choices*] That is the reward and blessing. If we make more good choices than bad choices, we are more likely not to physically hurt ourselves or others. We are less likely to be mean to others, so we will have good friends and relationships with people.

What can we learn from Noah? If we want to be godly, we must choose to know and obey God's directions.

COMMENT BOX

■ ■ ■ ■ ■ ■ ■ ■ ■ ■ ■ ■ ■ ■ ■ ■ ■ ■ ■

THINK: What went well as you taught this lesson? What can you do better?

_____

_____

_____

_____

_____

_____

_____

_____

TIP: Sometimes choosing child volunteers can be tricky. You do not want your lesson to fail because the child you chose does not cooperate, gives the answer away, etc. Before a lesson that involves kid volunteers, pray about who would be best to help you. Think through the activity and decide which child has the best personality to do that particular job. Also, try to rotate the opportunities to volunteer so a large number of the children get to participate throughout the year.

16 BEING ON MISSION TAKES EFFORT

■ ■ ■ ■ ■ ■ ■ ■ ■ ■ ■ ■ ■ ■ ■ ■ ■ ■ ■ ■

What is our purpose in life? What was the purpose of Jesus? Helping our children know what Jesus' mission was is a step in the right direction on the narrow path of godliness. {Deuteronomy 5:32}

Scripture Focus: Luke 4:17-19, Luke 22:42, Isaiah 61:1-2

Materials:

Do what God's teaching says: don't just listen and do nothing. When you only sit and listen, you are fooling yourselves.

—James 1:22, ERV

FUTUREFLYINGSAUCERS.COM

- Building materials such as large plastic connecting bricks, blocks, etc.

- Make a list of all the actions Jesus is reported as doing throughout the book of Luke. Section headings in a Bible make this easy. There will be 15-20 actions.

- Find a few biography books or videos about missionaries or other leaders in the church or society over the years. See a list on the Resources Page.

- James 1:22 poster

I used plastic bricks. Divide children into groups of three or four. Give a pile of equal amounts of building materials to each group.

Background: Jesus returned to Nazareth at the beginning of His ministry. He was surrounded by people who knew Him. He went to the synagogue on the Sabbath, but this time it was different.

OBJECT LESSON

■ ■ ■ ■ ■ ■ ■ ■ ■ ■ ■ ■ ■ ■ ■ ■ ■ ■ ■ ■

{Tell the groups that you are going to give them one to two minutes to work with their teams to build a cross out of the supplies. Warn them that you will be coming around trying to destroy their work. They will need to work together to build, protect, and possibly rebuild. If they get a cross built, they will need to protect it!

As the kids work, go around and "tear down" their creations. You could also "steal" some of their supplies. I had two other adults help me. This activity was loud. The kids really got into protecting their crosses!

After the time, see what progress has been made.}

{Ask and allow answers:}

- Were you given a mission, or a job, to do?

- Was it simple or complicated to build the cross?

- What made it difficult?

- What emotions did you feel as the activity went on?

- Did you ever want to quit?

- Why or why not?

BIBLE LESSON

Jesus was given a mission. In Luke 4, Jesus was given a scroll to read and He read the prophecy from Isaiah 61.

{Read Isaiah 61:1-2a}

After Jesus read these Scriptures, He told those who were listening that the prophecy was fulfilled.

{Ask:}

- According to these verses, what was Jesus' job? [*Preach the good news, heal the brokenhearted, tell about freedom to captives, provide freedom for sinners, proclaim the year of the Lord.*]

Did He do these things? It is important to look for the evidence if someone is claiming that he fulfills a prophecy.

{Go through the list of Jesus' actions. I wrote them on the board. As you read through them ask, "Did Jesus do this? Does it fulfill the prophecy from Isaiah?"}

{Ask:}

- Were these easy things that Jesus did? [*No*] No, in fact while He was in the Garden of Gethsemane before He was arrested, He asked God to take the cup of suffering away from Him. Jesus did not want to go through the awfulness of what He knew was coming, but He put His desires to the side and chose God's will instead.

- Could Jesus have walked away? What if He had gone through the Passover meal and then said, "*Later, men! I am out of here!*" and disappeared? Could He have done that? What if He decided not to go to the cross? What if Jesus changed His mind and said, "*You know what, Pharisees? You are not worth My time.*" Could Jesus have chosen not to die on the cross at any time? [*Yes, He could have left us.*]

However, He did not leave because He loves us.

Jesus had a mission to bring liberty to captives—freedom to those who have no freedom. We are the prisoners. We are prisoners to our sins.

{Ask:}

- Did Jesus finish His mission? [*Yes*]

- Was it easy? [*No*]

- Was it hard work? [*Yes*]

- Was it frustrating sometimes? [*Yes*]

- What did He do to finish His mission? [Died on the cross]

But Jesus did the mission anyway.

LIFE APPLICATION

You have been given a mission. Many times kids think, *"I am just a kid. What can I do?"* God used Samuel. God used David. He can use you, if you let Him!

Every person has been given a specific mission. Your job as a young person is to learn. You are to learn in school and at church. You are to learn your skills. You are to learn what you enjoy doing the most. God will then teach you what you are to do for Him, and He will use what you love and the skills you have developed to glorify Himself.

However, your mission will not be easy. Don't think you are by yourself in this. In fact, you can learn from those who came before you. We have all of the people we learn about in Scripture, but then there are others we can read about to see how God has used them and their mission.

{Pull out the missionary books and videos you collected. Show the covers and mention the names. Tell a little about each person's mission, but do not tell the whole story. I had kids asking me for books and videos when the lesson was over!}

{Hold up the poster. Read it aloud.}

If you worship with other believers in church, read your Bible, learn from your parents, and listen to your Bible teachers, but then do nothing that the Bible tells you to do, you are wasting your time. **You have a mission, and that means you must DO what God wants you to do.** There is a time for everything—a time to learn, a time to sleep, a time to play, a time to eat, a time to work hard. Working hard takes effort. Jesus worked hard at His mission and was successful.

We can do the same thing. So let's work hard!

What can we learn from Jesus and His mission? If we want to be godly, we must choose to work hard and put effort into doing our mission well.

COMMENT BOX

█ █

THINK: What went well as you taught this lesson? What can you do better?

_____

_____

_____

_____

_____

_____

_____

_____

TIP: People who have no vision or purpose perish (Proverbs 29:18). The same can be said about children. Bible teachers, whether parents or in a church setting, must teach children that they have a purpose and a mission given to them by God. When kids realize that God wants to use them and that there is a reason why things happen to them, they are more apt to stick with their relationship with Jesus and weather the storms of life.

17

HOW TO DEAL WITH CHEATING

■ ■

Cheating! Cheating comes in different forms, but each example oozes with dishonesty. Being able to choose honesty over cheating will help our children take a step in the right direction on the narrow path of godliness. {Deuteronomy 5:32}

Scripture Focus: Genesis 25; Genesis 27; Genesis 29:1-20

Materials:

- Picture of a weasel (See Resources Page.)

- Proverbs 11:1 poster

FUTUREFLYINGSAUCERS.COM

Dishonest scales
are detestable
to the Lord,
but an accurate
weight is His delight.

—Proverbs 11:1 (HCSB)

Background: Abraham, Isaac, and Jacob are the patriarchs of the Jewish and Christian faiths. They were sinful people. However, God chose to use imperfect people to bring about His perfect plan. Abraham was given a promise from God. He passed this promise down to his only son with Sarah, Isaac. Then Isaac was to pass the promise down to his oldest son. His oldest son was named Esau. But wait...the lineage does not go: Abraham, Isaac, and Esau. The promise was given to Esau's brother, Jacob. Why?

OBJECT LESSON

■ ■

{Ask:}

- What is a weasel? [*Allow answers*.] **{Show picture of the weasel. Every time a person in the narrative acts like a weasel, hold up the picture.}** A weasel is a small rodent that is long and narrow. This little animal is able to go halfway into a hole, change directions, and come right back out again.

- If I were to call a person a "weasel," would that be a good thing or a bad thing? [*Bad*]

- Why? [*Allow answers; lead answers to the conclusion that a person who says one thing and then does another, or cheats, could be called a weasel.*]

{Encourage the kids not to call people weasels or any other bad names. Be sure not to call the men from the Bible "weasels." Instead, say that they "acted like a weasel." You want to model not calling names, but still get the point of the lesson across.}

BIBLE LESSON

The Bible is filled with people who were not perfect. But there was one who really acted like a weasel. In fact, he acted like a weasel and eventually was out-weaseled by another person who acted like a weasel!

Jacob and Esau were twin brothers. Isaac was their father. In Biblical times, and even in some cultures today, a father will pass on a blessing, or inheritance, to the eldest son. The younger sons might receive a little something, but for the most part, the oldest would own everything from the father.

Jacob acted like a weasel. He wanted Esau's birthright. One day Jacob cooked stew and Esau came home from hunting. Esau was starving and dramatically asked for food from Jacob. Jacob seized the opportunity and told Esau he'd give him food only if Esau gave Jacob his birthright.

Esau agreed.

Perhaps Esau really was starving, but to give up one's birthright for food does not make sense. But Esau did, and Jacob took it.

Later Jacob had the opportunity to work with his mom to steal Esau's blessing. Not only did Jacob act like a weasel, but Rebekah, his mom, did too, in this situation. Jacob pretended to be Esau, received the blessing from his blind father, and ran away once Esau figured out what had happened.

Jacob ran away to his uncle Laban's house, where he fell in love with Rachel. Jacob agreed to work seven years for Laban so he could marry Rachel. The day of the wedding came. The marriage took place. In Biblical times, and still in some cultures today, the bride's face is totally covered during the wedding. That is what happened with this marriage. After the ceremony was completed, Jacob found out that his uncle Laban had acted like a weasel as well. Laban had given him Rachel's sister, Leah, to marry!

Jacob agreed to work another seven years for Laban, and he went ahead and married Rachel. Marrying more than one woman happened often in the Bible, but God does not recommend it. (1 Corinthians 7:2)

LIFE APPLICATION

■ ■ ■ ■ ■ ■ ■ ■ ■ ■ ■ ■ ■ ■ ■ ■ ■ ■ ■ ■

Jacob acted like a weasel. He was dishonest and selfish. He was a cheater and a coward. But God uses messed up, broken people to bring about His perfect plan! Hearts CAN change. Jacob did change.

If you read the Scripture, Jacob actually had a heart change ON THE WAY to Laban's home. Jacob had an encounter with God, and usually when that happens, a person is changed forever. However, with Jacob, it was not until he encountered God one more time that he was forever changed.

You must have an encounter with God as well. Hopefully, you will respond to God the first time, and not be like Jacob. You may not act like a weasel, but you have other sin in your heart. The Bible tells us that we all have sinned. That includes you and me.

{Tell your testimony about your encounter with Jesus here.}

Just because our heart changes does not mean we get out of consequences. Jacob had to go through even more trickery by his uncle, and he eventually learned never to cheat people again. When Jacob finally left Laban's house, he still had to deal with Esau and ask for forgiveness. Even though Jacob acted like a weasel at first, God used him to bring about the family from which Jesus would eventually come.

{Hold up the poster. Read it aloud.}

During Bible times, merchants would use balance scales to weigh money or items they were selling. If a merchant was dishonest, he would cause the scales to not be honest. Then he would make more money by cheating and stealing from the person buying.

{Ask:}

- What does the Lord think about that? [*It is detestable and gross; it makes Him sick.*]

- What delights the Lord? [*Accurate scales*] If you were a merchant with accurate scales, then you were honest.

What can we learn from Jacob? If we want to be godly, we must choose to be trustworthy.

COMMENT BOX

■ ■

THINK: What went well as you taught this lesson? What can you do better?

_____

_____

_____

_____

_____

_____

_____

_____

_____

_____

_____

TIP: If you have a balance scale, show it to the children. Explain that there is a knob or lever that keeps the scales accurate. The Bible is what keeps all of us accurate and pleasing to the Lord.

18 ENCOURAGING COOPERATION

■ ■ ■ ■ ■ ■ ■ ■ ■ ■ ■ ■ ■ ■ ■ ■ ■ ■ ■

Parents and teachers will agree that life flows much more smoothly with children when there is a sense of community and cooperation. Encouraging cooperation will help our children take a step in the right direction on the narrow path of godliness. {Deuteronomy 5:32}

Scripture Focus: Ecclesiastes 4:9-12, Exodus 17:8-13

Materials:

- A broom handle or walking stick

- Chair (student-size)

- Ecclesiastes 4:9-10 poster

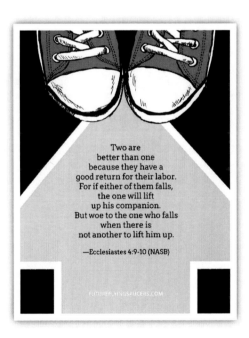

Two are better than one because they have a good return for their labor. For if either of them falls, the one will lift up his companion. But woe to the one who falls when there is not another to lift him up.

—Ecclesiastes 4:9-10 (NASB)

FUTUREFLYINGSAUCERS.COM

Background: Moses had led the Israelites out of Egypt. The people grumbled because they had no food, and God sent manna from heaven. They grumbled again because they had no water to drink. Moses went to God about this and was told to strike a rock. He did, and water gushed out—enough for all the people to drink. Then the Amalekites attacked...

OBJECT AND BIBLE LESSON

{Choose 3 volunteers. Have one be "Moses." Have "Moses" hold the "rod" (broom handle) horizontally. While "Moses" is holding it, read Exodus 17:8-13. You are doing this so the arms tire.

Be sure to explain the meanings of the word *prevail* and the phrase *hands were heavy*. "Moses" should be having a hard time holding up the rod. Ask the other two volunteers to stand on either side and help hold the arms of "Moses." Give "Moses" a chair to sit in.}

{Ask:}

- Was it hard to hold the rod up by yourself? [*At first it was easy, but then my arms started getting tired.*]

- Do you think you could have held that rod up for a whole day? [*No*] Moses couldn't either.

- Who were his friends? [*Aaron and Hur*] Aaron was Moses' brother, and Hur was Caleb's son. Both helped Moses lead the Israelites.

- Was it easier to hold the rod once you sat down and had help? [*Yes*]

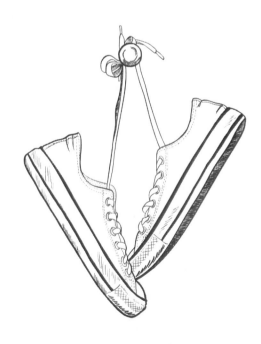

LIFE APPLICATION

■ ■ ■ ■ ■ ■ ■ ■ ■ ■ ■ ■ ■ ■ ■ ■ ■ ■ ■

Cooperation is important. No one can go through life alone.

One of the things that might happen to people when they are in jail or at a prison camp is something called **solitary confinement**. This is when a prisoner is placed in a room by himself for an extended amount of time. The prisoner is not allowed to have any dealing with people except when given food and water. It is awful. Many prisoners end up losing their minds or becoming irrational thinkers.

People are meant to be in community with each other. God wants us to get along and cooperate with each other.

{Hold up the poster. Read it aloud.}

{Ask:}

- What are some examples of cooperating with other people? [*Allow answers. Some examples could be: sharing, working on projects with others, not being stubborn and wanting your own way all the time, helping someone up if she has fallen or gotten hurt, playing on sports teams, giving clothing and food to those who might not have any, etc.*]

What would have happened if Aaron and Hur had decided they did not want to cooperate? Maybe they had other things to do. Instead, they were sensitive to the needs of their friend who needed them. They walked up the hill with Moses and stayed with him during the battle.

Success comes from working as a team. Some people think they can do everything all by themselves, but this is not what God wants. He wants us to help each other and cooperate so people can know about Jesus.

Can you think of a friend who might need your help? Go help him! Make sure he is not by himself, and cooperate so everyone can win.

What can we learn from Aaron and Hur? If we want to be godly, we must choose to cooperate and help others.

COMMENT BOX

■ ■

THINK: What went well as you taught this lesson? What can you do better?

_____

_____

_____

_____

_____

_____

_____

_____

_____

TIP: It is important to have cooperation between teachers as well. Make sure you have an assistant to help you carry the teaching load and deal with possible behavior issues. If you are a parent, cooperate with your children at times. Help them learn how to negotiate in a safe environment. You may find that they have some neat ideas!

19

BE AN ENCOURAGING PERSON

■ ■ ■ ■ ■ ■ ■ ■ ■ ■ ■ ■ ■ ■ ■ ■ ■ ■ ■

People struggle with life every day. Sometimes we are too busy to pay attention to those around us. Helping our children know how to encourage others during difficult times is a step in the right direction on the narrow path of godliness. {Deuteronomy 5:32}

Scripture Focus: Joshua 1:1-9

Materials:

- A *Choose Your Own Adventure* book (These books allow readers to make choices for the characters and create stories as they read. You can find one at your local library. I chose one that did not have aliens or things that could be scary, like ghosts or kidnapping. I chose *Grand Canyon Odyssey* and read a few portions aloud.) See Resources Page for examples of the book.

- Isaiah 41:10 poster

Do not fear,
for I am with you;
do not be afraid,
for I am your God.
I will strengthen you;
I will help you;
I will hold on to you with
My righteous right hand.

—Isaiah 41:10 (HCSB)

FUTUREFLYINGSAUCERS.COM

Background: The end of Deuteronomy tells us about the death of Moses. His death was a HUGE deal. Think about it. All of those Israelites knew only one leader. Those who had been in Egypt had died in the desert. This was a new generation of people who were ready to possess the Promised Land. Their leader died. Now what?

OBJECT LESSON

{Hold up the *Choose Your Own Adventure* book.}

Choose Your Own Adventure books are neat to read. A story begins and then the characters end up having to make choices that change their circumstances. As the reader, you get to make the choices for the characters, turn to the numbered page for that choice, and then read to see the consequences of the decisions.

{Read the "Warning!" page of the book. Then proceed to read a little bit of the story to get to a choice. Tell the kids the options and have them vote on a choice. Follow through with whichever choice they make. Allow this two to three times, but if possible, do not finish the story. Make it a cliffhanger!}

Did you know that your life is a "choose your own adventure" story?

BIBLE LESSON

Every person has a story. It is a great story.

Joshua from the Bible had a great story, too. Moses died, and Joshua took over the leadership of Israel. Not only was he to lead the people, but he was to lead the people into the Promised Land and conquer the land. Joshua realized that God was asking him to do a hard thing. Moses had been an amazing leader, a courageous leader. He had been greatly used by God.

Joshua might have been intimidated by what God was asking him to do. The first chapter of Joshua tells us that **God encouraged Joshua**. God knew He was asking Joshua to do some hard tasks. God wanted Joshua to know that He would be with him. Joshua would not be alone. Listen to God's words:

{Read Joshua 1:6-9 ESV if possible.}

How encouraging!

God told Joshua these things:

1.   Be strong and courageous!

2.   You will get the land.

3.   Be strong and courageous!

4.   Be careful to follow the law. Do not go to the right or the left!

5.   Meditate on the law day and night.

6.   Do these things and you will be successful!

7.   Be strong and courageous!

8.   Do not be frightened!

9.   Your God is with you wherever you go.

Joshua's life and the things God did with him were amazing! Joshua and the people DID conquer the land. Joshua WAS successful in all he did when he followed God's law and walked in His ways. God gives us the same encouragement.

LIFE APPLICATION

{Hold up the book.}

{Ask:}

- Think about this book. How does it work? [*As we read, we choose what decisions are made or what happens to the characters*.]

As you live life, you make decisions. In fact, every day you make decisions. Some are small and are of no real consequence, such as choosing to eat cereal instead of eggs. However some choices have great consequences. For example: choosing not to keep up with your backpack and losing your school stuff, or being disrespectful to your parents. Different situations have different consequences.

God is with you everywhere you go, hoping you will choose the right choice so you will have successful consequences. Verse 7 says: "Do not turn from it to the right hand or to the left, that you may have good success wherever you go."

{Ask:}

- Do not turn from what? [*God's law*]

- Where do we find God's law? [*In the Bible*]

- What should we do so we know what the law is? [*Read the Bible.*]

- Will reading the Bible mean we will always be successful? [*Allow for answers, and then explain that we will fail—in our eyes and in the world's eyes—at times. However, if we really are following God's ways, we will **not** fail at what GOD wants us to do.*]

God is giving you the same encouragement that He gave Joshua:

1. Be strong and courageous!

2. Do not worry. I have an amazing plan for you!

3. Be strong and courageous!

4. Stay in My Word and follow it! Meditate on it!

5.   Be strong and courageous!

6.   I will be with you wherever you go!!

{Hold up the poster. Read it aloud.}

If God gives us this kind of encouragement, and we desire to be godly people, that means we must give this same encouragement to OTHER people.

{Give an example of people who have encouraged you in your own life.}

{Ask:}

- Did Joshua have an easy time clearing out all those people from the Promised Land? [*No*] Absolutely not! He had to guide thousands of men into battle.

- Was it Joshua who made the walls of Jericho fall? Was it Joshua who made the sun stand still? [*No*]

God asks us to do hard and seemingly impossible things so HE can glorify himself and make His name known.

Making decisions can be hard. Encouraging others in our lives means we need to be intentional and look for those who need encouragement. Be strong and courageous! God encourages you. Now you go and encourage someone else.

What can we learn from Joshua and God's message to him? If we want to be godly, we must choose to be encouraged and encourage others.

COMMENT BOX

■ ■

THINK: What went well as you taught this lesson? What can you do better?

_____

_____

_____

_____

_____

_____

_____

_____

_____

_____

TIP: Help your children to be intentional with encouragement. Have them choose one person to pray for during the week. Have them ask God to show them how they can encourage those people. Then have them ask for the boldness to obey what God reveals.

20 WHY DO WE NEED TO BE GODLY ANYWAY?

■ ■

Why do we need to be godly? Does God really care about our choices? This Bible lesson focuses on the wide gate vs. the small gate. It will help our children understand that Jesus is the one and only gate. This is THE step in the right direction on the narrow path of godliness. {Deuteronomy 5:32}

Scripture Focus: Matthew 7:13-14; John 10:1-18

Materials:

- A real or toy gate (See Resources Page for a picture of a gate, if needed.)

- Poster board or a white board

- Deuteronomy 5:32 poster

So you shall observe to do just as the Lord your God has commanded you; you shall not turn aside to the right or to the left.

—Deuteronomy 5:32 (NASB)

FUTUREFLYINGSAUCERS.COM

OBJECT AND BIBLE LESSON

■ ■ ■ ■ ■ ■ ■ ■ ■ ■ ■ ■ ■ ■ ■ ■ ■ ■ ■ ■

{Show the gate or picture of the gate.}

{Ask:}

- What is this? [*A gate*]

- Why do we use gates? [*To go through fences easily; to keep something inside a fence; to not allow something to get into a fence*] We can walk through gates. We can close them. We can lock them. They can protect us or something we have inside a fence. Gates and fences can separate land, such as separating your yard from someone else's yard.

- Should you climb over fences? [*Probably not, especially if the property belongs to someone else*] Going over a fence you are not supposed to means you are trespassing, and that is against the law in some places.

In the book of Matthew, in chapter 7, Jesus was almost to the end of His Sermon on the Mount.

{Read Matthew 7:13-14.}

Jesus described two objects for us. Let's draw a picture of what He said.

{Draw a long fence. Put a small, narrow gate on one half and a broad, wide gate on the other.}

If there are gates, that means there is a fence, and the property on the other side belongs to someone else. So we have to choose a gate to get to the other side. The way through the wide gate is broad and it leads to destruction.

{Draw a wide path that leads through the gate and to an area of fire. Show many circles that can equal people on the wide path. Add the words DESTRUCTION and MANY.}

{Ask:}

- Which gate does Jesus tell us to go through? [*The narrow gate*]

- Why? [*It leads to life.*]

{Draw a person standing at the fork in the road. Add the narrow road going through the narrow gate. Have it lead to trees and smiley faces. Add some rocks on the road. Show only a few people on the road. Add the words *LIFE* and *FEW*.}

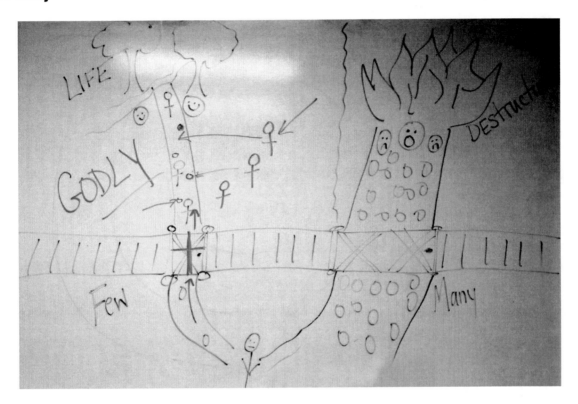

{Ask:}

- Which path will most people choose? [*The wide path*]

- Is it an easy path or a hard path? [*Easy*]

The narrow path has some potholes and rocks. Jesus tells us that the road through the narrow gate is hard. You have to decide which path you want to take.

If you choose a path, how do you get through the gate? John 10 helps us to know that answer. There are many things from the verses we could add to our picture. We will focus on verse 9. Jesus tells us that He is the door.

{Ask:}

- Which gate, or door, is He? The narrow one or the wide one? [*The narrow gate*]

{Add a cross inside the narrow gate.}

Jesus told us to ENTER through the narrow gate. He says that He IS the gate. He is the door. We enter the gate by allowing Jesus to be our Master. When we surrender everything to Him, then we walk along the narrow road.

{Ask:}

- If we DO NOT choose to have Jesus as Master of our lives, which gate or door do we chose? [*The wide one*] That road leads to destruction.

- How many people will choose Jesus? [*Not many*]

- How many will NOT choose Jesus? [*Lots of people*]

LIFE APPLICATION

Once you choose to have Jesus as your Lord and Savior, and you really mean that in your heart, you walk through that narrow gate. The problem is that there are times when we do not live as Jesus wants us to live and we start walking off the path. When we walk off the path, we end up hurting ourselves and those around us.

{Add people walking off the narrow path toward destruction. Draw a line between the people and the road to destruction.}

{Hold up and read the poster.}

{Ask:}

- How do we stay on the narrow path? [*We do what God commands us to do.*]

- When we turn to the right or the left, what ends up happening? [*We start going toward activities that hurt us and others.*]

When we turn to the right or the left, that is when we are making selfish choices and not living as God wants us to. Even though we might make poor decisions, once we have walked through the narrow gate, we can never go back to the broad road. **{Point to the line.}**

When we start to make foolish choices, God tries to get our attention so we will get back onto the narrow path. Sometimes we are convicted of our wrongdoings, and the Holy Spirit reminds us how we really should be living. Then we choose to walk on the narrow path again. (John 14:26, Isaiah 30:21, Joshua 1:7)

{Draw arrows showing the people going back to the narrow road.}

Sometimes God tries to get our attention and we choose to ignore Him.

{Ask:}

- What will happen if we make this choice? [*Consequences that might hurt us or others*]

- Does God care about our choices? [*Yes*]

- All of them? [*Yes*]

- What about choosing a red pencil instead of the blue pencil? [*Maybe not this type of choice*]

God loves you so much, and He cares about all of the daily choices you make. The choices that matter most are the ones that are based on God's commands. Does God say, "*You must always use a red pencil?*" No, but He does say to use words to tell others about Him. He tells us to say nice things about others.

It is our living out God's commands that keeps us walking on the narrow road to godliness. It is our faith that helps us step over the rocks and potholes in the narrow road.

The narrow road is hard. But Jesus says He walks with us every step of the way. When we die and we see Jesus face to face, He will tell us, "*Well done, good and faithful servant.*"

What can we learn from the wide and narrow gates? If we want to be godly, we must remember that Jesus is the way to life, and that by surrendering to Him we are agreeing to do everything that God commands.

COMMENT BOX

■ ■

THINK: What went well as you taught this lesson? What can you do better?

_____

_____

_____

_____

_____

_____

_____

_____

_____

_____

TIP: Pictures can be used to teach great truths. Challenge your children to read John 10 and add more to the main picture.

ALIVE IN CHRIST CHRISTMAS LESSON

What does the term *fellowship* mean? What about *Immanuel*? Here is a simple Christmas salvation object lesson that will help our children understand both of those terms.

Scripture Focus: Romans 8:10-11, Genesis 2:7

Materials:

- Plastic model animals (I used a lion, zebra, giraffe, and bear. Make sure you have one animal that is usually not seen in groups.)

- Dollhouse people (parents and children)

- John 3:3 poster

Jesus replied, "I assure you: Unless someone is born again, he cannot see the kingdom of God."

—John 3:3 (HCSB)

Background: While in the Garden of Eden, Adam and Eve had a perfect fellowship with God. They walked daily with God. Once sin entered the world, that fellowship was broken, and God took it upon Himself to get rid of sin so the relationship between Him and man would be healed.

The nation of Israel was the channel by which God used to bring about Jesus' birth.

OBJECT LESSON

■ ■

{Ask:}

- Do you know what fellowship is? [*Allow for answers*.]

Think about animals for a minute.

{Hold up the lion, zebra, and giraffe.}

Lions live with lions. Giraffes live with other giraffes. Zebras gather in herds with other zebras.

{Hold up the bear.}

What about bears? They do not really travel together in groups, but bears are friendlier to other bears than to other animals. Mama bears take care of baby bears, but not baby squirrels.

{Ask:}

- What about God? [*God is Spirit*.]

- Who does He live with? [*Allow for answers. The kids will probably say He lives with people, but you want them to answer that He lives with another "spirit."*]

BIBLE LESSON

When God created the world, it was only God the Father, Jesus the Son, and the Holy Spirit. God created Adam and Eve and placed them in the Garden of Eden.

{Ask:}

- What made Adam and Eve different from all of the animals? [*Genesis 2:7 tells us that God **breathed** into man and he became a living being.*] When God created people, He breathed into Adam and Eve to give them life. He did not do that with the animals.

{Hold up the dollhouse people.}

The serpent spoke to Eve and told her she would not really die if she ate the fruit of the Tree of Knowledge of Good and Evil. He deceived her.

{Ask:}

- What was the choice that Adam and Eve made? [*They ate fruit from the Tree of Knowledge of Good and Evil.*]

- Did their bodies die? [*No*] No, but the spirit that had been breathed into them did die. (James 2:26) Adam and Eve died spiritually and started to live according to the flesh. (Romans 8)

{Have the dollhouse people lie down.}

God can only live with spirit, remember? So He had to tell Adam and Eve to leave the garden.

As soon as sin entered the world, God started a plan to get His people back to Him. The wages of sin is death, but God wanted fellowship with His people. He wanted to live with them.

The Old Testament tells us over and over again different things God did to get His people back. He created the Law. He created the Tabernacle. He created the Temple and sacrifices. However, people could not do what needed to be done to make their spirits alive again. The people could not be righteous enough.

A prophet named Isaiah said a strange thing in Isaiah 7:14. He told the people that a virgin would have a baby and that the name of that baby would be Immanuel. That word means *"God with us."* This was strange because, in those days, the place to be with God was at the Temple or the synagogue.

In Bethlehem, God allowed His Son to be born as a baby. His name, Jesus, means *"God saves*." However, that is not the name Immanuel, is it? The angel Gabriel told Mary to name the baby "Jesus" because God was bringing salvation, which would allow Him to dwell and live with his people once more. Jesus is God (John 10:30). Therefore, when Jesus lived on the earth, God dwelt with His people. That means *"God with us! Immanuel!"*

LIFE APPLICATION

{Hold up the dollhouse people.}

Each person has a sin problem. Every person is born of the flesh. Sin causes us to die and not have a relationship with God. Not having a relationship with God means being spiritually dead. We cannot do anything to get our spirits alive again. God has to fix that problem.

{Hold up the poster. Read it aloud.}

A man named Nicodemus went to Jesus. Jesus told him that unless you become born again, you cannot see the kingdom of God. Nicodemus, confused, asked, *"How can I re-enter my mother and be born again?"*

Jesus told Nicodemus that he had to be born of water and of the spirit. Ahha!! Being born of the water from a mother is the flesh. But our spirit must be reborn as well!!

How does this happen? When you believe that Jesus is who He claims to be, you must act on that belief. That is being saved or born again. Will you really allow Him to be your Master? Will you really obey Him? Are you sorry for the wrong things you have done? Do you want to please God?

If you do believe that Jesus lived, died on the cross, and rose again, then Jesus saves you from being just flesh and dead. Then the Holy Spirit comes inside of you. He **dwells** with you! I don't understand how all of that works, but I have experienced Jesus dwelling in me, and I know being born again is real and it is good! I have NEW LIFE!

{Read Romans 8:10-11.}

This equals fellowship! God with us! Immanuel!

Do you believe in Jesus? Perhaps you know Jesus exists, but He does not dwell with you. You have not been born again. When you know with your whole being that Jesus dwells or lives in you, you act differently. You walk and talk with Jesus. You introduce Jesus to your friends. You gather with other people who know and dwell with Jesus. You read about Jesus so you can know more about Him.

Are you doing those things? Or are you still spiritually dead and in the flesh?

Christmas is a great time to learn more about Jesus and to really think about what He did when He was born in Bethlehem.

Jesus is a great God. I urge you to dwell with Him today!

{Give the children an opportunity to respond to the Holy Spirit. You can lead them in prayer or invite those who want to ask more questions to come and talk with you. See the Extra Resources section if needed.}

COMMENT BOX

█ █

THINK: What went well as you taught this lesson? What can you do better?

_____

_____

_____

_____

_____

_____

TIP: When presenting the gospel, always allow children to come to you to ask questions about salvation. However, some children "follow the group." If you have multiple children come to you at once, ask each child in the group individual questions about why he or she came to you. Have them explain the gospel back to you. If they are unable to articulate why they need to speak with you, you can be pretty sure that those children might be following a friend or not really understanding what is going on. If that happens, tell the children, _"I can tell that God is working on your heart and teaching you about Himself. You keep listening and learning. When you are ready, I know you will come to talk with me again."_ You can then send those children back to the main group. This will help you figure out who is serious about receiving the gift of salvation.

EXTRA RESOURCES

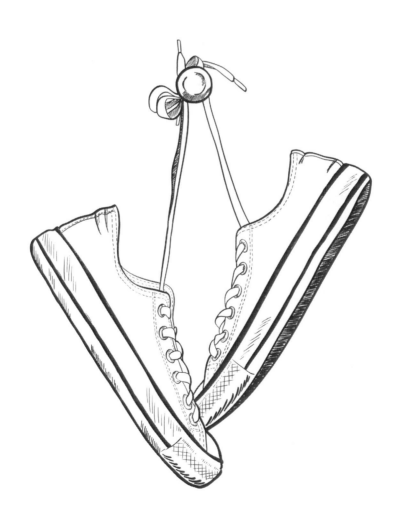

HOW TO LEAD
A CHILD TO CHRIST

■ ■

After you teach a Bible lesson, there are times when it is necessary to ask the children if they want to receive the gift of salvation through Jesus. Always have those who want to make some sort of decision leave the larger group of kids. I do this by either having them stay behind while the others leave, or taking the small group into another room. I do this because it causes the child to physically make a decision: *"Do I stay? Or not?"* This also allows for fewer distractions. (Always be sure to have another adult nearby. That's a safety rule!)

Ask many questions; you want the children to think through what they are doing. These questions should not be answered by "Yes," "No," or "Jesus." Use lots of Scripture, because you want God's Word to be working.

There is no minimum age for salvation. Even three-year-olds can recognize they are sinners and be sorry for what they do. However, you do want to be sure that the child, no matter the age, understands this lifelong commitment.

Salvation is a big deal, and you don't want a child to make a decision that is not understood or taken seriously. If at any point you sense that there is confusion or uncertainty on the child's part, say, *"I can tell that God is working in your heart. I want you to keep listening and learning."* Then dismiss that child who is not ready.

Examples of Counseling Questions:

1. Why have you decided to talk with me?

2. Why do you need Jesus as your Savior?

3. What is sin?

4. What are some examples of sin?

5. Can you do anything to get rid of sin?

6. Read Romans 3:23.

7. Who is Jesus?

8.   What did Jesus do for you?

9.   Read 1 Corinthians 15:3-4.

10.   Read John 3:16 or Acts 16:31.

11.   Would you like to pray to God and receive Jesus now?

If the child understands the questions and is answering appropriately, describe salvation as a heart change—a choice to move away from sin and toward God. If the child is serious about dealing with sin and wanting to live for Jesus, explain that he or she needs to talk to God and that talking to God is called prayer.

At this point lead the child in prayer. Have the child copy what you say or tell the child what information should be included when asking God for salvation:

• Admit to God you are a sinner.

• Say that you are sorry for those sins. Ask for forgiveness.

• Tell Jesus you believe Jesus is God's Son and that He died on the cross and rose again.

• Confess that Jesus is your Lord and Master.

• Thank God for saving you.

Once the child has prayed, read Hebrews 13:5b and 6a. Ask, *"What has Jesus done for you?"* This will give assurance of salvation.

Pray for that child when you are finished. Then have the child choose at least one person to tell about what happened (usually a parent).

Rejoice with the family!

It is possible you might have a situation that includes parents who are not happy about the choice made by their child. If this happens, explain the decision to the parents, but then, if at all possible, disciple that child yourself. If the child goes to another church or no church at all, check on the child when you can. Definitely pray for that young Christian.

Be sure to tell your pastor of the child's decision so he can follow up with the family and discuss baptism. If you are a parent and your child has accepted Jesus as his or her Savior, be sure to help your child grow in knowledge and service.

HOW TO BECOME AN EXCELLENT BIBLE TEACHER

■ ■

When teaching children, our goal is two-fold. First, we want kids to **get right** with God through a saving faith. Second, we want our children to **stay right** with God through the sanctification process.

> You, however, continue in the things you have learned and become convinced of, knowing from whom you have learned them, and that from childhood you have known the sacred writings which are able to give you the wisdom that leads to salvation through faith which is in Christ Jesus. All Scripture is inspired by God and profitable for teaching, for reproof, for correction, for training in righteousness; so that the man of God may be adequate, equipped for every good work.
>
> 2 Timothy 3:14-17 (NASB)

WHAT We Want to Teach:

We want to focus on verse 16, because if we can (1) **teach** doctrine in such a way that reveals sin, and then (2) explain how to stop sinning (**reproof**), and then (3) counsel children how to fix their sin problems (**correction**), THEN (4) they will be restored to a character of **righteousness** so God can use them for good works. This is the cycle of sanctification after salvation.

However, the cycle of sanctification does not revolve in a circle. It is more like a spiral as we grow closer to God and He works on our hearts.

We can also think of it this way: As our view of God increases, our view of ourselves decreases. (Sounds like John the Baptist!) The discrepancy is seen more and more. Jesus becomes bigger in our lives the more we know of Him. He must increase. We must decrease. Yes, we are children of God, heirs to a kingdom, but we are clothed in unrighteous rags. We need Jesus.

This is what we want for our children, whether they are our own or those we teach in the church. **We want them to view Jesus as being the One and Only Greatest Person in their lives.**

HOW We Teach This:

In order to be an excellent Bible teacher, a person must seek God first and foremost. **I fail at this.** I am not an excellent Bible teacher because of what I do, but because of what God chooses to do through me. I attempt to read the Bible every day. I attempt to make good choices. I mess up.

I think this is what makes the difference between a mediocre Bible teacher and an excellent Bible teacher: **An excellent Bible teacher daily recognizes his or her own need for a Savior**.

It is through our failings that Christ shines His light into our Bible lessons. When we explain to children how God is real, forgiving, and personal in our own lives, they will begin to search for that type of relationship as well.

How do we teach children? By allowing God to teach us. This means we need to take an honest look at ourselves, evaluate our hearts, and apply what God shows us to our teaching.

Prayerfully read through the next few questions and answer them.

Evaluation of Yourself:

1. Are you sold out to Jesus?

2. How enthusiastic are you about your teaching?

3. Are you interested in your children's lives?

4. Can you sense the needs of your children?

5. Are you a servant leader?

Evaluation of Each Bible Lesson:

1. Did you accomplish your objectives?

2. If not, why?

3. What was weak?

4.   What was strong?

5.   What changes should you make before the next lesson or before you teach this lesson again?

Evaluation of the Teaching Year:

1.   How many salvations took place among your children?

2.   Can you see a growth of Biblical knowledge in your children?

3.   Was there growth in their spiritual heart knowledge?

"To whom would He teach knowledge,
And to whom would He interpret the message?
Those just weaned from milk?
Those just taken from the breast?
"For He says,
'Order on order, order on order,
Line on line, line on line,
A little here, a little there.'"

Isaiah 28:9-10 (NASB)

Biblical knowledge, or learning the Scriptures, takes a life time. It involves a little truth here and a little lesson there, step by step. We Bible teachers want our children to discover for themselves what they *ought* to do, so that through loving God, they will *obey* Him regardless of any obstacles. **A committed will to obey God equals a changed life.**

A NOTE FROM THE AUTHOR

■ ■ ■ ■ ■ ■ ■ ■ ■ ■ ■ ■ ■ ■ ■ ■ ■ ■

Friend, I encourage you. You hold the living, powerful Word of God in your hands. Use it wisely. Read it lovingly. Teach from it enthusiastically. Love powerfully. **Be Excellent!!**

Your Servant,

Anne Marie

FutureFlyingSaucers.com

COLORING PAGES

The one who
follows instruction is
on the path to life,
but the one who
rejects correction
goes astray.

—Proverbs 10:17 (HCSB)

But no man
can tame the tongue.
It is a restless evil,
full of deadly poison.
We praise our Lord and Father
with it, and we curse men who are
made in God's likeness with it.
Praising and cursing come
out of the same mouth.
My brothers, these things should
not be this way.

—James 3:8-10 (HCSB)

FUTUREFLYINGSAUCERS.COM

Truly, I say to you,
to the extent that you
did it to one of
these brothers of Mine,
even the least of them,
you did it to Me.

—Matthew 25:40 (NASB)

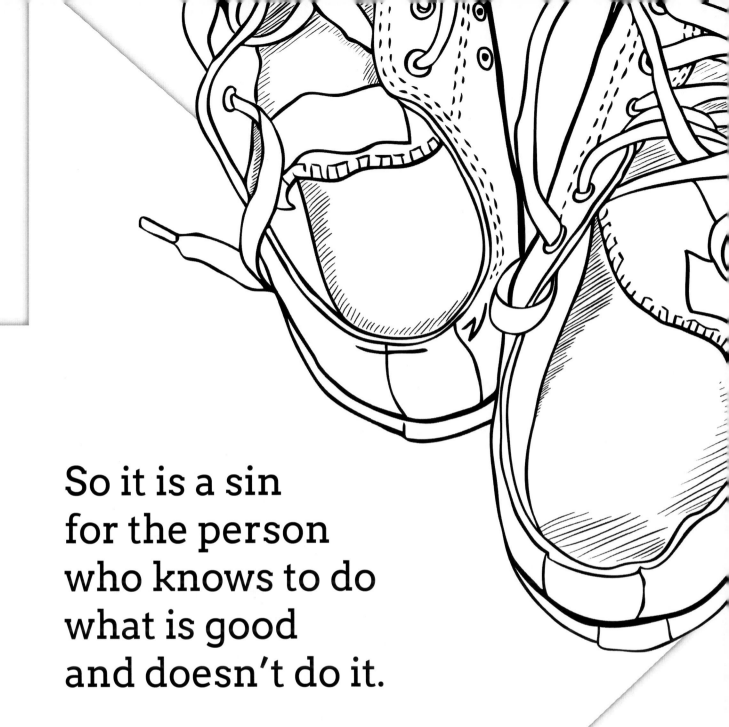

So it is a sin
for the person
who knows to do
what is good
and doesn't do it.

—James 4:17 (HCSB)

If it is possible,
as far as it
depends on you,
live at peace with
everyone.

—Romans 12:18 (NIV)

No temptation
has overtaken you
that is not common to man.
God is faithful, and he will not
let you be tempted beyond
your ability, but with the
temptation he will also provide
the way of escape,
that you may be able
to endure it.

—1 Corinthians 10:13 (ESV)

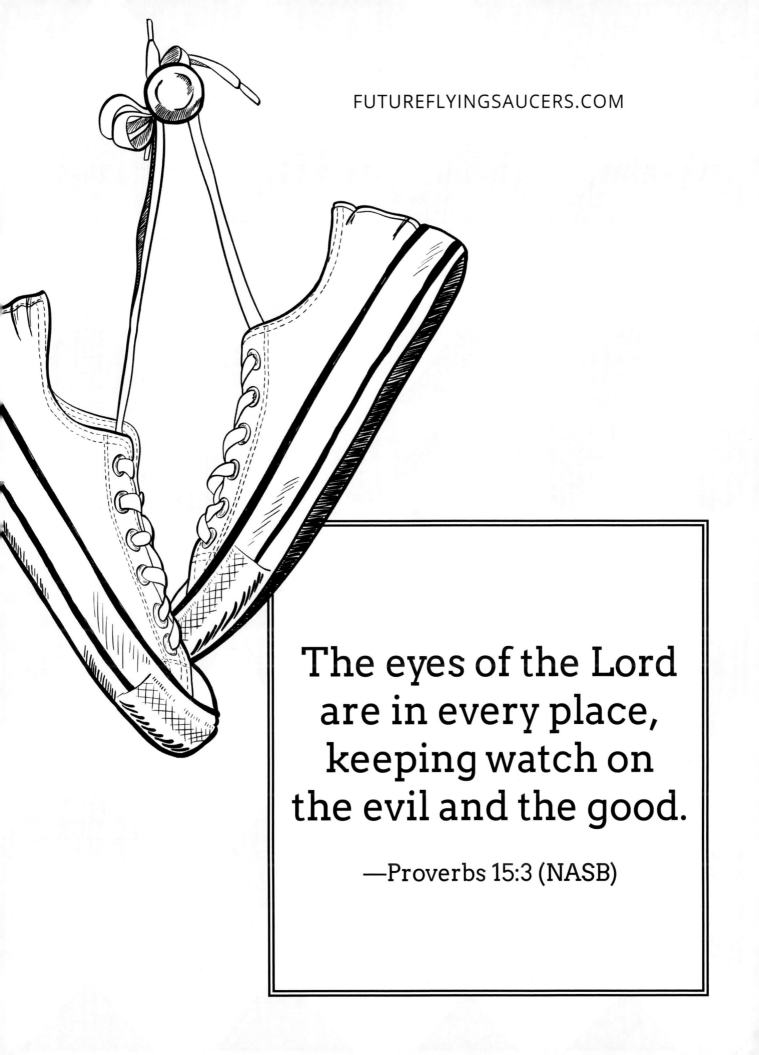

The eyes of the Lord
are in every place,
keeping watch on
the evil and the good.

—Proverbs 15:3 (NASB)

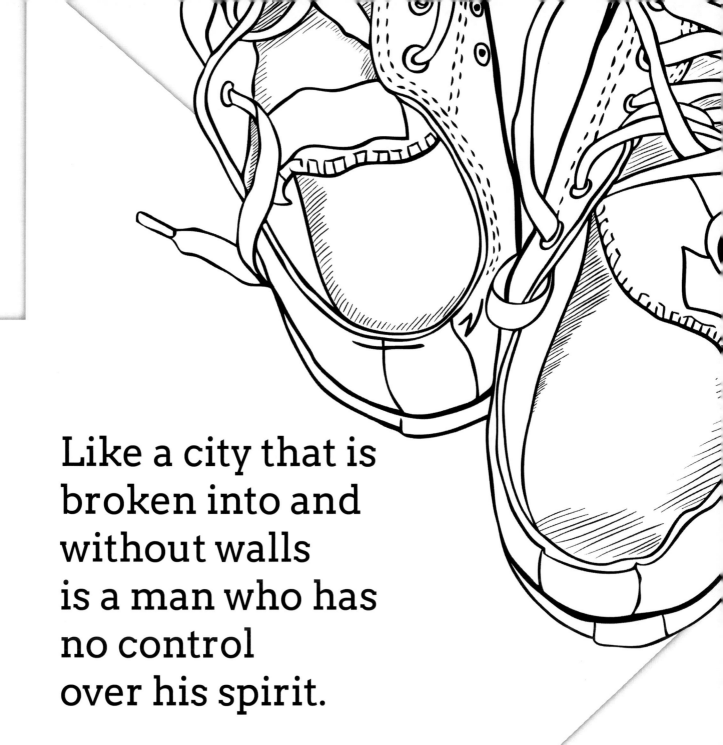

Like a city that is
broken into and
without walls
is a man who has
no control
over his spirit.

—Proverbs 25:28 (NASB)

For the whole
Law is fulfilled
in one word,
in the statement,
"You shall love your
neighbor as yourself."

—Galatians 5:14 (NASB)

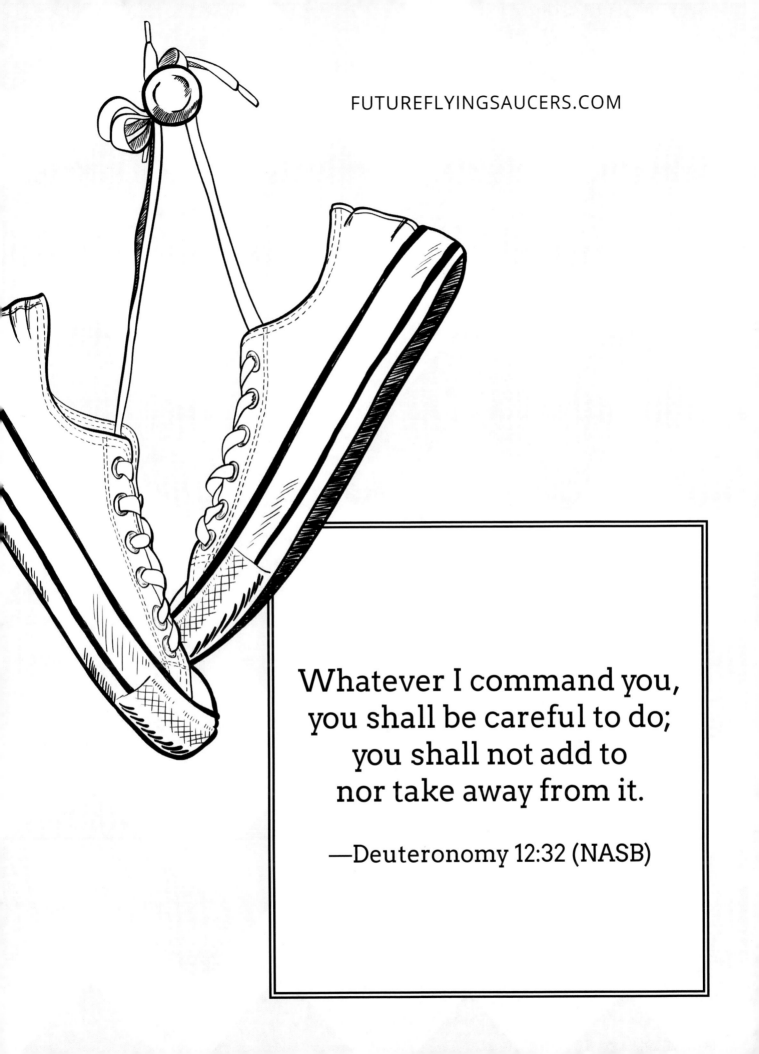

FUTUREFLYINGSAUCERS.COM

Whatever I command you,
you shall be careful to do;
you shall not add to
nor take away from it.

—Deuteronomy 12:32 (NASB)

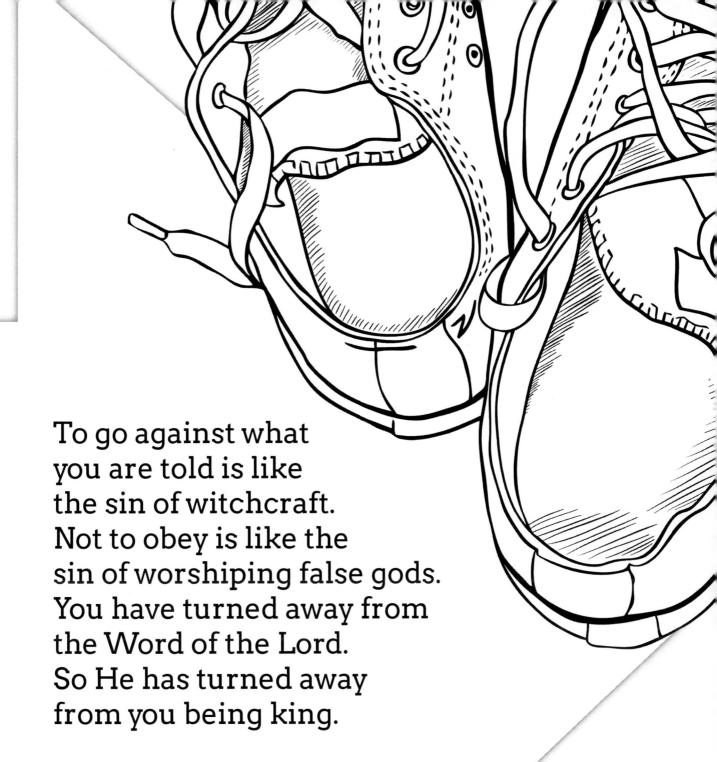

To go against what
you are told is like
the sin of witchcraft.
Not to obey is like the
sin of worshiping false gods.
You have turned away from
the Word of the Lord.
So He has turned away
from you being king.

—1 Samuel 15:23 (NLV)

Brothers, consider your calling:
Not many are wise from a
human perspective, not many powerful,
not many of noble birth.
Instead, God has chosen what is
foolish in the world to shame the wise,
and God has chosen what is weak in the
world to shame the strong.
God has chosen what is insignificant and
despised in the world—what is viewed
as nothing—to bring to nothing what is
viewed as something, so that no one can
boast in His presence.

—1 Corinthians 1:26-29 (HCSB)

FUTUREFLYINGSAUCERS.COM

Love is patient
and kind. Love is
not jealous, it does
not brag, and
it is not proud.

—1 Corinthians 13:4 (ICB)

Greater love has
no one than this,
that one lay down
his life for his friends.

—John 15:13 (NASB)

My son,
don't forget my teaching,
but let your heart
keep my commands;
for they will bring you
many days, a full life, and
well-being.

—Proverbs 3:1-2 (HCSB)

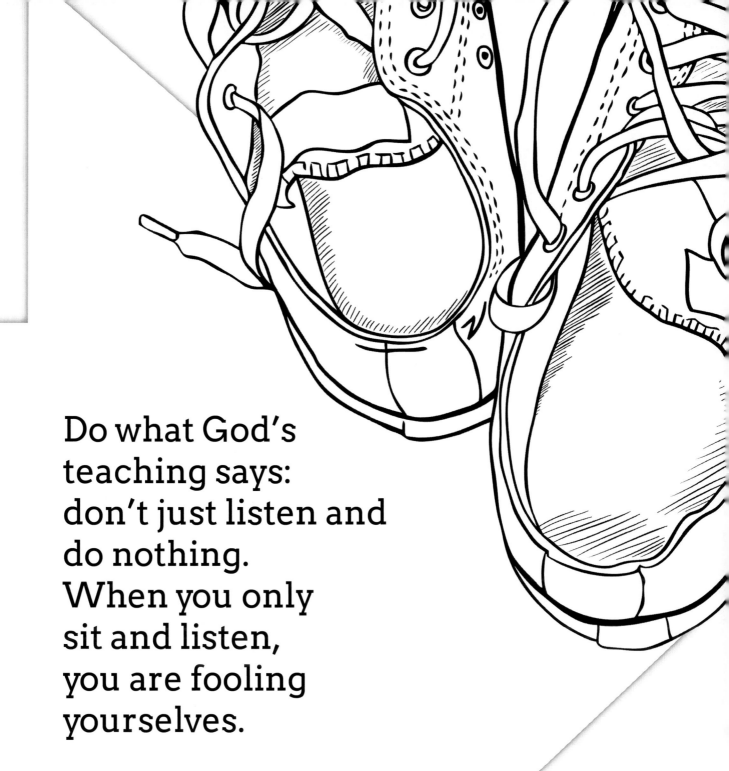

Do what God's teaching says: don't just listen and do nothing. When you only sit and listen, you are fooling yourselves.

—James 1:22, ERV

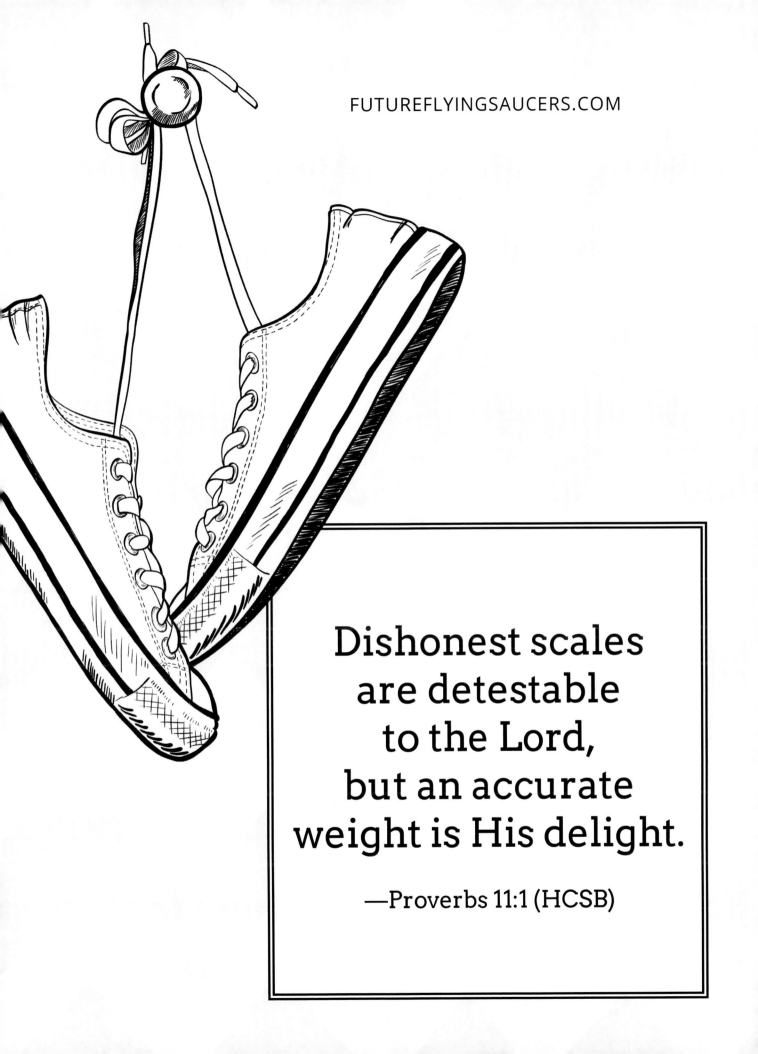

FUTUREFLYINGSAUCERS.COM

Dishonest scales
are detestable
to the Lord,
but an accurate
weight is His delight.

—Proverbs 11:1 (HCSB)

Two are
better than one
because they have a
good return for their labor.
For if either of them falls,
the one will lift
up his companion.
But woe to the one who falls
when there is
not another to lift him up.

—Ecclesiastes 4:9-10 (NASB)

Do not fear,
for I am with you;
do not be afraid,
for I am your God.
I will strengthen you;
I will help you;
I will hold on to you with
My righteous right hand.

—Isaiah 41:10 (HCSB)

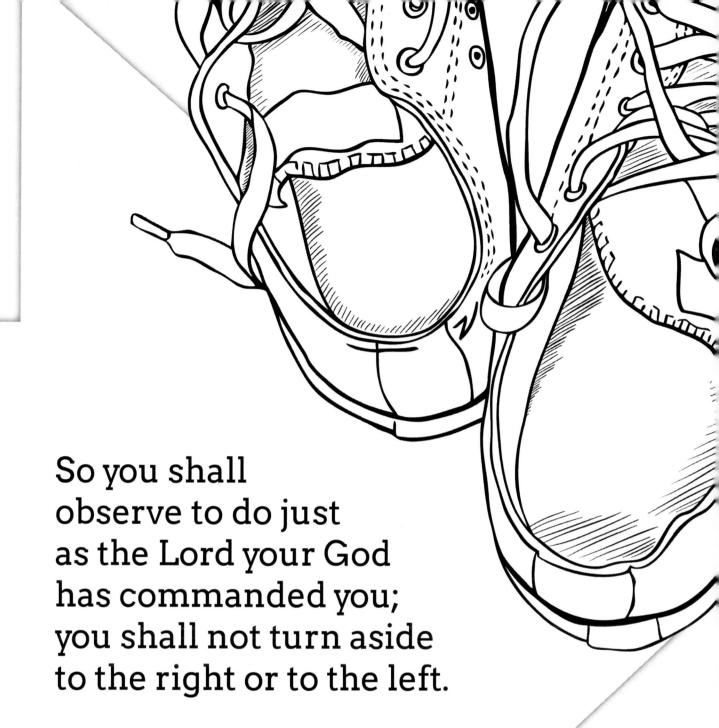

So you shall observe to do just as the Lord your God has commanded you; you shall not turn aside to the right or to the left.

—Deuteronomy 5:32 (NASB)

Jesus replied,
"I assure you:
Unless someone is
born again, he cannot see
the kingdom of God."

—John 3:3 (HCSB)

For more ideas, lessons, coloring pages, games, etc., go to my Pinterest boards. I've found all kinds of fun stuff for you!

Be sure to leave a **5 star review** on the website (Amazon, etc.) where you purchased this book.

Made in United States
North Haven, CT
06 February 2024

48395685R00104